"I took one companion on my journey - an old
French gentleman poodle known as Charley
. . . He is a good friend and traveling
companion and would rather travel about than
anything he can imagine. If he occurs at length
in this account, it is because he contributed
much to the trip. A dog, particularly an exotic
like Charley, is a bond between strangers.
Many conversations en route began with 'What
degree of a dog is that?' "

JOHN STEINBECK
Travels with Charley
© 1961, The Viking Press, Inc.

D1418105

PROTECTING

YOUR PETS
(at home and away)

by Hal Gieseking

Gieseking & Clive, Inc.
Bronxville, New York

SF415.45
G5

Acknowledgements

To Carol Parmes for her extensive research which made this book possible.
To Bruce Larkin for mapping out the dog and cat vacations.
To Linda Florio for her editing and writing contributions.
To Fay Brisk for her help and encouragement.
To Betty Oechsli for her secretarial ability in bringing it all together.

And to these veterinarians who contributed important information and ideas:
Dr. C. G. Ziegler, Baltimore, Maryland
Dr. Gary R. Smith, New Rochelle, New York
Dr. Cosmo Ferraro, Chicago, Illinois
Dr. W. C. Jamison, Los Angeles, California
Dr. Harold Durham, Detroit, Michigan
Dr. Richard G. Pearce, Detroit, Michigan

Bob Clive, Designer

Robert C. Gold & Associates, Production

© Copyright, 1979 by
Gieseking & Clive, Inc.
Box 716, Bronxville, N.Y. 10708

All rights reserved. Except for the inclusion of credited brief quotations, no part of this book may be reproduced or utilized in any form or by any means, electronic or mechanical, including photocopying, recording, or by any information storage and retrieval system without the prior written permission of the publisher.

Distributed to the trade by the
Berkshire Traveller Press,
Stockbridge, Massachusetts 01262

First Printing
Printed in the United States of America
Library of Congress Catalog Number: 78-65330
ISBN: 0-912944-53-6

*For Betty and Hazel
who love all animals,
and Danny who loves
all people*

Table of Contents

Many people develop a very special affection for a dog or a cat.

Maybe it's because pets have no ulterior motive when they sit next to you, although some cat owners might dispute that. Maybe it's because they display endless curiousity in what you're doing; activities that would bore a human audience to death, such as picking up trash or repairing a cabinet door.

Never mind how the feeling comes about, this bond between human and animals. It happens, and there's just no sense trying to explain it to a non-lover of cats and dogs.

But pet owners can get caught between two loves, the love of their pets and the love of travel. Or they own pets and must travel for business reasons.

Do you take the pet along?

Do you leave the pet with total strangers?

Or do you take the longest walk in the world—that walk that leads away from the kennel the first time you've left your pet behind?

Whether you travel or stay at home, how can you *protect* your pet from the growing problems of petnapping?

Actually a considerable body of information already exists which would help pet owners cope with all of these problems. But it's scattered in esoteric magazines published for various animal groups, or buried in 700-page animal health texts that seldom get read.

That's why this book was written, to gather in one place all of the pertinent information that would help pet owners choose kennels or pet sitters carefully—or go traveling with their pets with the fewest number of problems.

This book is based on a number of interviews with animal health authorities, all of whom are not always in agreement. In most cases we have presented the viewpoint of the majority.

Because your pet's life and health are at stake, we have tried to be totally candid about the problems. As you will see in Chapter 5, there are still some possible problems when you ship your pet by air. We don't buy the airlines' contention that your pet travels in "passenger comfort"—unless they're talking about traveling masochists who prefer flying in a crate, in a dark area surrounded by boxes, luggage and lettuce heads.

We have tried to make this a working book that you can refer to whenever you have a particular question.

Scattered through the book are drawings by Dick Kline, the man who invented the paper airplane that he flew on CBS' "60 Minutes" and the "Mike Douglas Show." Dick's drawings have a Thurber-like innocence that we felt would encourage the whole family (young and old) to get involved with "Protecting your pets" and absorb useful information as painlessly as possible.

We hope you enjoy this book and find that it provides practical help. And next time a non-petlover scoffs at your concern for animals, think how nice it is that such affection can still exist between humans and animals in a world of terrorism and general callousness.

1

HOW TO DECIDE - SHOULD YOUR PET TRAVEL WITH YOU OR STAY AT HOME

There is still no better way to make a decision than to follow the practice of Benjamin Franklin. Whenever he had an important decision to make, he would write all of the reasons why he *should* do something on one sheet of paper, and all of the reasons he *shouldn't* on another. Then he weighed both cases and made his decision.

Here are some of the reasons that you may want to put on your "YES" list when deciding whether or not to travel with pets.

1. Pets can be good company, particularly on long drives.

2. Pets are a link to strangers. Part of the real pleasure of travel is meeting new people and discussing different viewpoints. However, many people are basically shy and never find a way to start conversations with strangers in another city. But a friendly dog or nosy cat can do wonders in breaking the ice. John Steinbeck used his French poodle Charley for just such a job. "In establishing contact with strange people, Charley is my ambassador. I release him and he drifts toward the objective, or rather to whatever the objective may be preparing for dinner. I retrieve him so that he will not be a nuisance to my neighbors—et voila! A child can do the same thing, but a dog is better."*

3. You *know* your pet is all right because it is traveling with you. You don't have to worry whether a pet you left behind has stopped eating or has run away from home with a canine/feline lothario.

4. You save kennel or pet sitter costs.

5. A large dog can be a deterrent to crime.

Travels with Charley, The Viking Press, Inc.

How to decide

6. Your pet is a member of the family and deserves a vacation as much as the rest of the family. Sometimes more.

However, before you rush off to pack your pet's suitcase, you should jot down any reasons why your pet *shouldn't* go traveling.

1. A pet is a continuing responsibility and sometimes a nuisance. It may hold you back from some activities. For example, if you're driving across country, you may have to skip some attractions because you don't want to leave your pet for a long period in an overheated car.

2. Your pet should not travel if:
   - Under six months of age
   - An older cat or dog (past five years of age) unaccustomed to traveling
   - Pregnant
   - In heat
   - In poor health
   - Very nervous or hyperactive in strange situations

3. Traveling with pets can be expensive. Sending a 150-lb. Great Dane by plane from New York to Amsterdam can cost you as much as $293.70.

4. Your pet will face certain new dangers, such as poisons, or diseases common to areas you'll be traveling through.

5. Some pets react to changes in diet or water with stomach upsets which include vomiting and diarrhea, hardly a "Wish-you-were-here" situation.

Whichever you decide—thumbs up or thumbs down on traveling with your pet—there are some practical ways for a pet owner to cope successfully with either decision. Read on.

2

HOW TO CHOOSE A CLEAN, SAFE KENNEL

Choosing a clean, safe kennel

Some thirty years ago if you checked into a motel, it would frequently be a dowdy "tourist cabin" with a bare bulb hanging from the ceiling. If you took your dog to the kennel, it might simply be some crates behind a barn.

The motel and kennel industries have come light years since those days. According to Jim Krack, Executive Director of the American Boarding Kennels Association (the kennel industry's only trade association), "A modern kennel today costs anywhere from $100,000 to $1,000,000 to construct. When this kind of investment is involved, you know kennel owners are motivated to manage the business carefully and take good care of pets."

There are now thousands of kennels all over the U.S. Most of them fall into these general categories:

The luxury city kennel. These usually have "cute" names such as "Doggy House" or "Purr Inn." Because of local noise ordinances, they frequently do not have outside runs. Instead they house your pet in individual enclosures which they call "suites." Many of the amenities are clearly designed to appeal more to the masters than to the pets. There may be off-the-floor beds with mattresses, a separate carpeted living room area (which incidentally is harder to disinfect than cement flooring), a "gourmet" chef, and even toy telephones. Many self-respecting sporting dogs would throw up if exposed to all this anthropomorphic nonsense. But it may be the perfect setting for a pampered house pet who has spent little time with other animals or in outdoor settings. The pets are usually released into exercise areas (by themselves) twice a day. Some of the prices are beginning to match those of human vacations. Depending on the size of your pet, you could spend anywhere from $7-$15 a day for this resort luxury.

The country kennel. These kennels stress outdoor "country club" living in kennels which frequently have regal-sounding English names such as "Glen Oaks" or "Kensington Acres." Many of these offer long outdoor runs and are particularly good for larger dogs that require a great deal of exercise daily. Prices at these country kennels are usually lower than in the city, often in the $5-$10 a day range. Prices are always based on the size of your pet. Cats are cheaper to board than dogs.

There are many variations in between, stretching from the city to the suburbs and country areas. These include veterinarians who take in pets, animal hospitals, and pet stores. Many pet experts recommend against boarding your pet with veterinarians or at animal hospitals. The problem is that your pet may be exposed to sick animals.

Should you board your pet?

Some veterinarians and animal health groups are not always enthusiastic about the boarding experience for animals: They recommend the home environment (with pet sitters) as the best solution. But others say that boarding kennels have improved so much in recent years that you can safely board your pet if you choose the kennel carefully.

However, there are some pets that do not belong in a kennel. As a rule of thumb, if your pet is over five years of age and has never been to a kennel before it probably will not adjust easily to kennel life. Sick animals should never be taken to kennels because you risk infecting other animals, and your pet will not get the constant attention that would be provided in an animal hospital. Dogs under six months of age should not be put in a kennel. Cats can be a special problem. Many cats are very choosy about their friends, and other cats and dogs are not always on the welcome list. In such cases you may have to leave your cat at home with a sitter or choose a kennel which has a quiet, isolated section especially for cats.

Another consideration is whether *you* feel comfortable about putting your pet in a kennel. Some pet owners walk through a Dante's inferno of guilt when they walk away from the kennel the first time. If they hear so much as a whimper that might have come from old Rex, they're ready to call the whole vacation off. The only cure for these guilt pangs is to leave your pet in the kennel for only very short periods of time, such as a weekend, until you are sure that both your pet and you can live with the experience.

Choosing a clean, safe kennel

Some problems you should know about

Anyone who checks a dog or cat into a kennel should know about certain problems that can occur. Many occur in some of the best-run kennels and are not the fault of the kennel owner.

1. Your animal may lose weight. Larger animals can drop as much as ten pounds during a kennel stay. Some pets pine for their owners and must be coaxed back to eating. Others who have been confined to apartments or who have not been around many animals suddenly become superactive. They literally become weekend athletes, running constantly up and down the runs chasing animals in the next-door runs. That also accounts for why some pets return home and seem to sleep for a week. Some owners have accused kennels of tranquilizing their sleepy returnees when the potion was really a week of vigorous running.

2. Your dog may return with a case of infectious bronchitis, also known (to the kennel owners' chagrin) as "kennel cough." This dry cough should be treated promptly by a veterinarian. There is very little a kennel owner can do to keep this air-borne virus from spreading, except keep germicidal lamps going 24 hours a day. Best bet is to protect your dog with a vaccination which is now available for kennel cough. This vaccine is not 100% effective but does protect your pet against half the viruses that cause kennel cough. Cats may also contact respiratory diseases and should be protected by vaccination before kenneling.

3. Your animal may lose its housebreaking habits. particularly if the kennel experience is over two weeks long.

How to choose a kennel

Unfortunately this is a difficult job. There are no "seals of approval" awarded by any organization that could guide you. Some states have passed public health and animal welfare laws which supposedly govern kennel operation. However, in most areas enforcement is very weak. One kennel owner in an area where enforcement was supposed to be rigid said she had not been inspected in over three years. Others report that they pass the inspections simply by hosing down their front steps.

You may be surprised to know that there are no real standards for constructing a kennel. Anyone can decide to call himself a kennel owner. There are widely diverging opinions about how a kennel should be built. Kennel owners still frequently fight like cats and dogs about whether a run should have a gravel or cement floor, and how long pets should be alternately caged and exercised. There are some bad kennels around. These are usually run not by Simon Legrees, but by financially strapped owners who cut corners and staff—usually to the detriment of the animals they house.

The problem is compounded by the fact that some kennel owners, even good ones, will not let you inspect their premises. While some are obviously hiding filthy quarters, others are genuinely concerned that a constant flow of strangers keeps the animals upset and off their feed.

So what do you do? How can you make an intelligent choice of kennels under these conditions? Here are some suggestions:

• Ask your veterinarian for recommendations. Find out if he has personally inspected the kennel.

• Call the local humane society and ask to speak with the field officer. This person is usually charged with responding to complaints about kennels. Even if he can't give you specific recommendations, he can warn you about problem kennels.

• Call the A.S.P.C.A. and ask for recommendations.

• Ask friends who have had good boarding experiences with their pets for their recommendations.

With a list of possible kennels in hand, you're ready for the next important step.

Visit and inspect the kennel

Take along a note pad and make some notes.

The two most important things you want to check are cleanliness and the attitude of the staff toward animals. Your nose is a reliable guide to cleanliness. If the kennel smells bad, the staff is

Choosing a clean, safe kennel

not cleaning and disinfecting the premises properly—and that could mean serious trouble for your pet.

If the kennel will permit you to visit the area where the animals are kept, observe the following:

Are there individual water and food dishes in each of the enclosures? Are they clean?

Do you notice a number of flies in the kennel? This could be another indication of lack of cleanliness.

Are you comfortably cool in the area (if you're inspecting during the summer) or comfortably warm (during a winter inspection)? Ask a member of the staff if heating/air conditioning is maintained on a 24-hour basis.

Are there germicidal lamps burning in the kennel to reduce the possibilities of air-borne diseases (such as kennel cough)?

Watch the staff at work. If they seem to work at a frantic pace, it could mean the kennel is shorthanded and that your cat or dog will not be properly watched.

Look at the other animals. Do they seem healthy and alert?

Even if the kennel will not permit you to inspect the pets' actual quarters, you can still learn a great deal about the kennel by walking around the outside.

How well is the building constructed and maintained? Would you consider it a potential firetrap?

Do you notice piles of trash or loose garbage near the kennel? Give the kennel a black mark.

How high are the fences? Dogs do escape, either by vaulting low fences or tunneling. Dogs lost from kennels are seldom found.

How long are the outdoor runs? If the run is about 50 feet long, many dog experts feel that it will provide a large dog with plenty of exercise. Are the runs covered or otherwise protected from rain and snow? Does the run have a gravel or cement floor? Gravel keeps dogs from getting flat paws but is hard to disinfect quickly. Cement floor can wear down the pads on a dog's paws but can be easily disinfected. Ergo, if it's a show dog, choose a kennel with gravel runs. Check if there are cinder blocks between the runs or chain link fence. Chain link fences allow dogs to urinate on sleeping neighbors, not a very sanitary habit. Ask if the dogs are able to use the runs all during the daylight hours or are only admitted to the runs twice a day. (The latter is a common practice at many kennels that want to reduce heat loss through the entrace to the runs.) You may not *want* to let your pet have continuous access to the run—particularly if you're concerned about weight loss—but you should know what the kennel's policy is.

If you have a cat to board, ask to see where it would be kept. Ideally this would be in an area out of sight of the dogs. Cats, unlike dogs, do not need runs. They exercise isometrically by stretching in cages. Many cats seem to prefer their own private "den" to a "hail-hail-the-gang's-all-here" atmosphere.

Now have a talk with the kennel manager.

Ask if the dogs are kept in their own enclosure with a doorway to an outdoor run or in cages, If the kennel brochure says dogs are "hand walked," that's a good clue that the dogs *are* kept in cages and only let out twice a day. Some kennel owners defend the practice of keeping dogs in indoor cages. Said one, "Laboratory animals are kept in cages all of their lives, and they get along fine."

But Mr. Neil McLain, Administrative Director of the Baker Institute for Animal Health, Cornell University, disagrees. "Laboratory dogs that are born and bred in labs and dogs raised in the home from puppies are completely different animals that can't be compared. If I were looking for a kennel for my dog, I would certainly want more room and more exercise than a cage provides."

Ask to see the contract you will be asked to sign. Note one very important clause that is now being inserted in some contracts. "Five days after written request for removal of animal has been mailed to address on this card, the animal will be considered abandoned and may be disposed of, or sold."

The reason for this clause is the action of some irresponsible pet owners. They take unwanted pets to the kennel and leave a phony address. They believe the kennel will find a home for the animal when the owner doesn't show up. But the innocent also have to suffer because of these people. If your vacation or busi-

Choosing a clean, safe kennel

ness trip turns out to be longer than expected, *always* notify the kennel that you want to extend the stay of your pet. This could prevent the loss of your pet if the kennel can't contact you.

Ask the kennel manager about requirements.

Many kennels will not admit pets under six months of age. (Very young dogs should not be exposed to other dogs because they are in that dangerous in-between period when they have lost the natural immunity to diseases conferred by their mother's milk and they have not yet had a full complement of vaccination shots.)

If the kennel *demands* that your pet have all necessary shots before admittance, score a point for them. It shows that the kennel really cares about the pets already in the kennel.

Ask about the food the kennel will serve your pet. Some kennels will provide the same brand you are currently serving your pet. Others will serve a "standard" food to all pets, but may allow you to supply your own brand (at your own expense). If a "standard" brand is used, find out the name. Begin to switch your pet to this food several days before you take it to the kennel to be sure your pet will eat this food.

Ask if the kennel will give medication. Most will, for a small additional fee—usually around 50¢ a day.

Preparing your pet for the kennel

To be sure your pet has a good boarding experience, you may want to follow this checklist:

1. It's essential that you acclimate your pet to the kennel situation. Begin to take your pet to the kennel for short 1-2 day periods (after its 6-month birthday). The dog or cat quickly learns it has not been abandoned, and will adjust to this occasional experience. But the 4-years-old dog who has never been away from home in its entire life may react with genuine shock when thrust into a kennel while its owner disappears for a month. Animal experts have said that these are the animals most likely to get upset, eat poorly, and contact any disease other animals may bring into the kennel.

2. After you've selected your kennel, make reservations early. During peak travel periods such as the summer and holiday weekends, the best kennels may be booked up weeks in advance.

3. If you book your pet for a holiday period, always ask the exact hours the kennel is open. Some kennels may close at noon on the day preceding a major holiday.

4. Take your pet to the veterinarian for a general physical checkup and be sure all shots are up to date.

Most animal medical authorities agree that dogs should be vaccinated against:

> Distemper
> Canine hepatitis
> Leptospirosis (two types). Optional in some areas
> Kennel cough (infectious bronchitis)
> Rabies

All of these shots (several combined in a single injection) can be started at two months of age—with the exception of rabies vaccinations, which should not be given to puppies until they are at least four months old.

Booster shots are needed throughout the dog's life to maintain the effectiveness of these vaccines.

Cats should be protected by vaccination against:

> Feline upper respiratory diseases
> Feline distempter
> Rabies

Vaccinations can begin when the kitty is about eight weeks old, except for the rabies vaccination which should not be given until the pet is four months old. Booster shots throughout the cat's life are recommended.

5. Switch your pet to the kennel's "standard" food several days before you take it to the kennel. Any problems?

6. Put a collar on your pet with an attached name plate engraved with your name and address.

7. Assemble a small box of items you should take to the kennel—your pet's favorite toy, or a small piece of your clothing. An old sock of yours may convince Rex you're really hiding right around the corner. Also take along any medications, particularly heartworm tablets if the vet believes this is a problem in your area.

Choosing a clean, safe kennel

8. Give the kennel a sheet of paper with your veterinarian's name, address, and phone number. Also include your itinerary with addresses where you can be reached in an emergency.

9. Take off for a guilt-free vacation, convinced that you have done everyting possible to protect your friend in your absence.

P.S. If you arrive back home a few days early and want to leave your pet in the kennel while you catch up on chores, don't "visit" your pet. It stirs your pet up needlessly and may upset its acceptance of kennel routines. Just call to be sure that your pet has been eating all right and seems to be in good health.

NOTE: You may want to ask if the kennel belongs to the ABKA (American Boarding Kennels Association). This relatively new nonprofit trade association is interested in constantly improving the standards of kennel operation. Membership in the ABKA is one indication that the kennel owner is genuinely interested in learning more about animal welfare. If you have a dispute with one of the 500 U.S. and Canadian kennels that belong to the ABKA, this organization will serve as mediator. The address is ABKA, P.O. Box 7567, Colorado Springs, CO 80933.

Make holiday reservations early. The best kennels can be booked up weeks in advance.

3

HOW TO FIND
AND
'TRAIN' RELIABLE
PET SITTERS

If you do decide to leave your pet behind when you go traveling, the best place to leave almost all cats and most dogs is in your own home—with a pet sitter you trust.

There are three major advantages of this arrangement over boarding your pet in a kennel.

1. Your pet doesn't have to go through the trauma of adjusting to totally new surroundings.

2. You don't have to go through the pangs of guilt about leaving your pet in a strange place where it might refuse to eat or be exposed to diseases carried by other animals.

3. Your home will be occupied while you're away; a strong deterrent to burglaries.

However, finding a good pet sitter may require some effort. And helping the pet sitter do a good job requires a lot more effort than simply handing over the leash and the key to the house.

Ms. Mary Ellen Blizzard, co-owner of Pet Sitters, a professional pet-sitting service in New York City, personally interviews every candidate who wants to join her staff. "The most important qualification is that the person must truly love animals. When I interview someone, I have a cat and dog present. I want to see how the person reacts to the animals, and how *they* react to the person."

This is sound advice when you start looking for a sitter. The worst thing you can do is to foist a sitting job on someone who doesn't like pets. Sitter and pet will be miserable while you're away, and the sitter may become careless.

Where can you look for a sitter?

Neighbors may sometimes be willing to swap sitting services. You walk and feed their poodle while they weekend in Connecticut. They return the favor for your Siamese cat while you're out of town for a day. This casual swap is fine for a day or weekend, but not for extended vacations. You will want someone who will actually spend nights with your pet rather than simply feeding and walking them.

Relatives who have raised pets of their own are good candidates.

You can also find some good choices by calling Senior Citizens Centers in your area. Be sure, however, to match the sitter to the dog. If you have a Great Dane, it could be physically impossible for an older person to control.

You can also try an ad on college bulletin boards or call student employment bureaus on local campuses. A conscientious student could be a perfect sitter.

It's usually best not to advertise for a sitter in the general newspapers. You may attract some unwanted types, and you're also advertising the fact that you plan to leave town shortly.

After you've found your sitter, you should both sign a short letter of agreement. This is particularly important if the sitter is a relative stranger to you. The agreement should set the fee (usually on a per night basis). The sitter typically supplies his or her own food but has the run of the house. The sitter should also be given a "petty cash" fund to buy food or medications for the pet if necessary. You should specify in the agreement any other services you would need, for example, watering plants in your absence, answering the phone, etc.

Then you can give the pet sitter a short "training" course.

"I always invite the sitter into my home several days *before* I leave town," said Carol Sturm, a dog-owning writer who lives in Haydenville, Mass. "I want to be sure the pet sitter knows how to feed Duffy and give him his medication."

During this essential orientation period, you can answer any questions the sitter might have. You can also show the sitter where the pet foods and heartworm pills and other necessary medications are kept.

Let the sitter feed and medicate the pet while you are still there. He or she may need special instruction in giving pills. Many pills have to be split in half for the proper dosage. Some animals spit out pills as rapidly as you shovel them in. Show the sitter any tricks you've developed, such as rolling the pill in a ball of cream cheese.

Show the sitter any rooms the pet should stay away from, especially areas where you may store paint, household cleaning supplies, and insecticides. All of these can poison your pet.

Reliable pet sitters

Tell the sitter about any extra services you would appreciate while the sitter is living in your house, such as answering the phone and picking up the mail from outside boxes, and watering plants. Show the sitter where to put out garbage for pickups.

Go for a walk with your sitter and pet in areas you normally walk in. Warn the sitter about any hazards of the road, such as a German Shepherd in the red house who daydreams of taking a nip out of your pet.

While you're outside, show the sitter where an extra key to the house is hidden. (If the sitter lost one key, he could be locked outside with no way to get to your pet.) Have the sitter use the key to open the door and explain any "secrets" of a troublesome lock.

Be sure to give the sitter your personal itinerary, with addresses along the way where you can be phoned in an emergency.

This period of orientation can prevent many possible problems and will help you leave home with a totally clear conscience. You can use this checklist to simplify your briefing of the pet sitter.

Checklist for briefing pet sitter

1. Pet's food

A. Kind (brand name) _____

B. Quantity fed _____

C. How often? _3x a day_____

D. Normal feeding time _8, 12:5_____

E. Name and address of store in area carrying this brand____

_____

2. Exercise

A. Released in back yard? Yes X No___ How long? _____

B. Walks
   How long? __1 1/2 hrs__

   How many times a day? __3__

   Briefly describe walking route _____

   _____

C. Location of leash or harness

3. Medical

A. Name, address, phone number of veterinarian _____

_____

B. Medication
   Kind _____

   Dosage _____ N/A _____

   Frequency _____

   Name and address of store where additional medication
   can be purchased _____

C. Briefly describe any medical problems your pet may have
   and tell pet sitter how to cope with them. _____

   _____

4. Special instructions

A. Any rooms in house "off limits" to pet? _____

B. Any hazards for pet in or around house? (Example: Insecticides and rodent poisons in garage, dangerous household
   cleaning supplies—such as drain cleaner in basement) ___

   _____

Reliable pet sitters

C. Is pet allowed on any furniture? _____

5. **Pet's idiosyncrasies/habits** (Examples: Dog waits for someone to open front door and then runs away. Cat goes bananas and tears draperies when vacuum cleaner is turned on. Pet may not eat the first day the owner is away, etc.) __

6. **Household emergencies**

   Fire department phone number_____

   Police department phone number_____

   Name, address, phone of neighbor or family friend who can help in an emergency _____

   _____

   IMPORTANT: Brief sitter on location of smoke alarms, escape ladders, fire extinguishers.

7. **Extra services**

   A. Answering phone and taking messages. How do you want your phone answered? _____

   B. Water plants_____

   C. Pick up mail and newspapers from outside boxes_____

8. **Your travel itinerary and phone numbers where you can be reached.**

9. **Name and address of friend or relative who can be called in the event sitter can't contact you.**

NOTE: Please write all of this information on a separate sheet of paper. Give it to the pet sitter and discuss. It can prevent many problems and will do wonders for your peace of mind while you're away.

4

HOW TO TRAVEL WITH YOUR PET

Once you've definitely made up your mind to travel with your pet, you have a number of other important decisions to make that will affect the success of your trip. Preplanning is the secret of a good trip with pets.

How to travel with your pet

The major decisions:
When

The ideal seasons for pet travel in the U.S. are the spring and fall. If possible, avoid the summer months when your pet could face heatstroke. The summer is also heartworm season, a serious problem for all dogs who travel in mosquito-infested areas. Do not send your dog by air when the temperature is over 80°F. and the humidity is very high (90%–100%). If you do travel during the summer months, do most of your traveling early in the day before the temperature builds up.

Where

You now can travel literally any place in the world with your pet. However, your itinerary planning should be guided by certain restrictions currently in effect in many parts of the world. For example, your dog will be quarantined for six months on arrival in England. Your dog or cat will be quarantined for three months in Hawaii. Thousands of hotels and inns all over the world now accept pets but may place certain limitations on them. You may have to board your pet in the hotel's kennel, and because the number of animals that can be accommodated is limited you should book space weeks in advance.

Camping makes an ideal family and pet vacation. But don't let your pet run wild in the woods because of the dangers of other animals and hunters.

How

You have two primary choices of transportation, by car or air.
By car
This is the most popular way to travel with pets. But you must begin to accustom your pet to car travel early in its life if you want to take peaceful long vacation drives.
By air
Almost all airlines will ship pets in appropriate containers in the baggage compartments. Many airlines will also allow you to take a pet (in a kennel that fits under the seat) into the passenger compartment. Usually only one pet per flight is allowed in the First Class section and one in Economy Class. There are still some hazards when you ship your pet by air. These are discussed frankly in Chapter 5.

By ship

In the great old days of transatlantic travel by ship it was common to see a number of pet shipmates on board. But the number of transatlantic ships has dwindled to a precious few, and pets are barred from most cruises.

The Cunard Line's QE 2 still offers space to dogs and cats on transatlantic crossings, and the accommodations are posh. Pets stay on the Promenade Deck and can take the sea air on a walk to their own Edwardian lamppost. The animals are tended by kennelmates and may be visited and walked by owners during the voyage. (The pets are not allowed in cabins.) The cost is $145 for the first dog and, for some mysterious reason which a Cunard spokesman could not explain, $210 for a second dog. You would pay $65 for the first cat; $105 for the second. Note: Book one of the QE 2 voyages which stops first in Cherbourg, France (most of them do). Disembark in France because, as previously stated, if you go on to England on the ship, your dog will be impounded for six months.

By bus

Interstate bus lines in the U.S. bar all pets, except Seeing Eye dogs. Some intrastate and foreign bus lines will accept pets, but it may depend on the mood of the bus driver.

By train

AMTRAK has a prominent sign in Grand Central Station in New York which says invitingly, "ASK ABOUT OUR POLICY FOR PETS." When a reporter inquired what this policy was, the reservations clerk shouted, "I'll tell you our new policy. We don't take dogs. We don't take cats. Leave them home!" End of conversation.

The European railroad network is more tolerant. You can carry small pets (in carriers) "as long as the other passengers don't complain." You can even put a small pet in a bag, but if the head protrudes the pet must be muzzled. Larger dogs must ride in the baggage compartment in kennels. The fare is half of the Second Class fare to your destination.

Preplanning checklist

Here is a checklist you can use to make sure you don't forget something.

( ) **1.** Make hotel/motel reservations all along your itinerary. Verify that each currently accepts pets. If the hotel offers adjacent kennel space, reserve a spot for your pet.

(   ) **2.** Take your pet to your veterinarian for a complete physical checkup. Be sure all vaccinations are up to date. Tell your veterinarian where you plan to travel and ask if there are any special precautions you should take regarding your pet. Get a Veterinary Health Certificate and a Rabies Vaccination Certificate. Be sure the latter clearly indicates the *type* of rabies inoculation (Modified Live Virus vaccine, Killed Virus vaccine, Chick Embryo vaccine or Nerve Tissue vaccine). Each of these vaccines has different periods of effectiveness. That's why officials of various foreign countries and some states may ask you to name the type of inoculation your pet has received.

(   ) **3.** Check with foreign consulates about any new requirements for bringing pets into their areas. (See Chapter 10.)

(   ) **4.** If going by plane, make reservations for the passenger compartment or baggage compartment for your pet.

(   ) **5.** Buy a portable kennel for your pet. Let your pet gradually get used to this kennel and start sleeping in it at night.

(   ) **6.** Buy a good leash or harness and add a nameplate (with your name and address).

(   ) **7.** Make up a written itinerary. If you plan to stop at theme parks or other attractions along the way, write ahead to see if they have kenneling facilities. Many amusement areas are beginning to recognize the dangers of leaving pets in hot cars and are making kennel space available to visitors. These include Disney World, the Kennedy Space Center, Busch's Old Country in Virginia, the Toronto Zoo, and many others.

(   ) **8.** Consider buying pet medical care insurance. Many pet owners are unaware that you can buy such coverage now in the U.S. This is a policy that provides a set amount ($50 or $100 per accident) and about $100 for illness. It's very low cost and can take the expensive sting out of an unexpected accident or illness while you're traveling. The policy is so new that even your insurance broker may not know about it. Current underwriters of this policy include the American Universal Group, Paxton National Insurance Co. and Underwriters at Lloyd's London.

(   ) **9.** Pack your pet's bag. Bedding, medication, food, favorite toy, flea and tick preventatives, and required papers.

5

SAFEST WAY
TO SEND
YOUR PET BY AIR

Air travel

If you would have viewed TWA Flight 753 bound for New York on June 1, 1978 from the vantage point of a flying saucer, you might have thought the plane had been commandeered by a gang of dogs and cats. There in the First Class and Economy sections dogs and cats were happily coffee-tea-or-milking with the human passengers. Earlier the captain of the plane had noticed that something had gone wrong with the baggage compartment temperature. When he landed, he allowed passengers to rescue dogs and cats from this compartment and bring them into the passenger areas.

The quick action and compassion of the TWA captain is just one indication of how far the airline industry has come in its care of air-borne pets. Prior to Congressional approval of amendments to the Animal Welfare Act in 1976, the airline/shippers' treatment of pets could best be described as Middle Ages barbarism.

The industry's claim that animals traveled in "passenger comfort" was constantly punctured by true horror stories: puppies shipped in lettuce crates, animals left for days on a loading dock without food or water, and lost animals.

While conditions have improved considerably, various animal experts and airline executives were not in agreement by how much.

"The standards are still just barely minimal," said Fay Brisk, a dedicated animal rights crusader and former staff member of the White House Office of Consumer Affairs. "And airlines are still flying pets during hot periods when no animal should be flown."

An executive of an international airline, also a dog lover, was asked if he would send his pet in the cargo hold of his own airline. "No—and not on any other airline. I have just heard too many stories of problems."

But another airline executive who works right in the baggage/freight area of a large domestic airline said, "I honestly feel it's much safer to ship a pet by air now. We used to see a number of injured or killed animals at this airport. But last year we only saw about ten dead animals. We still have problems, especially with short-nosed animals which are very susceptible to heat. Another problem we haven't licked: Animals are still exposed to heat or cold on the long, slow drive to the planes on the baggage trucks. The kennels are also exposed to noise all the way. Sometimes these planes are two miles away from the freight receiving areas.''

We have talked with a number of airline and animal health experts and have reached these conclusions.

● It *is* much safer to send pets by air now, but there are still genuine risks. Some animals are still being lost. Others are being sent on hot, humid days when they should not fly. Some types of planes are not as safe as others because of temperature problems in the cargo holds. The DC-10 has been pointed out as a plane which is too warm for animals during summer months.

● You can greatly increase the safety of your pet if you follow some common-sense rules which are based on knowledge of how airlines ship pets. For example:
The safest way to send a pet by air is to take it on board with you into the passenger compartment. The pet must remain in the kennel during the flight, and you must put the kennel under the seat ahead of you during take-offs and landings. That means the kennel can be no higher than eight inches. Many airlines accept one pet in First Class and one pet in Economy Class. This is on a first-come, first-served basis, so you should make pet reservations as soon as your travel plans are set. Obviously only smaller pets can be accommodated in this way.

Other ways (in descending order of safety):

● Your pet travels with you as excess baggage. While your pet must travel in the cargo hold in a kennel, at least you are traveling with the pet and can minimize or eliminate any waiting time in cargo areas. If the airline will permit, take your kenneled pet directly to the airline gate and ask one of the airline personnel to put your pet on board. If you can possibly avoid it, don't let the kennel ride on the baggage conveyor belt (where accidents and jam-ups can occur). Book a nonstop or direct (no change of planes) flight.

This minimizes the number of times the kennel must be handled and reduces the risk of loss. (Everyone who has suffered through the lost luggage hassle knows that it can happen just as easily to kennels.)

• Retain a commercial shipper that specializes in pet transportation. These companies will pick up and deliver your pet to the airport, provide kennels, and generally look out for your pet all during the trip. They can also arrange overnight boarding en route on long trips. Two of the better known companies in this field are:

Canine Carriers
5 Brook St., P. O. Box 3271
Darien, Conn. 06820

(Call them toll-free at 800-243-9105 for an interesting free folder about their services.)

World-Wide Pet Transport
96-01 Metropolitan Ave.
Forest Hills, N.Y. 11375 (with agents all over the U.S.)
Phone (212) 544-8518

This company reports that it has never lost a pet during its five years in business.

• Send by regular air cargo. This is the least safe method, particularly if you're sending the animal overseas. Airlines frequently "bump" pet shipments. The reason is that kennels require a greater amount of space than the size of the box itself. There must be space around the kennel to permit ventilation and to give the animal air to breathe. During busy periods, the airlines could leave kennels sitting overnight while they load the cargo holds with more profitable freight. That is one reason you should *never* ship your pet during holiday periods. Even if your pet makes the flight, there is less likely to be enough ventilation and breathing space in a hold crowded with holiday shipments. Always pick up your pet as soon as you are notified that the plane has landed.

Here are some suggestions from people who have regularly shipped their pets by air.

1. Buy a shipping kennel in advance. (See *The ideal kennel* in this chapter.) Let your dog or cat become accustomed to staying in this kennel overnight. Feed and water your pet in the kennel. If you wait until the last minute and then thrust your pet in the kennel and take it to the airport, you greatly increase your pet's tension and fright.

2. Put a collar on your pet. The collar (as mentioned before) should have a plate on it with your name and address. But do not muzzle or leash your pet. A muzzle could choke a pet who became airsick. The pet also could become entangled in the leash and injure itself.

3. Avoid weekend and holiday air travel.

4. Do not fly with your pet or ship your pet by air if the temperature is over 80° F. and the humidity is over 90% (or 90°F. if the humidity is 50%).

5. Avoid airlines with labor problems. The classic technique (short of a strike) in the airline industry is the "rule book slow down." Recently, for example, the air controllers at La Guardia Airport in New York were protesting their contract by keeping planes taxiing along the ground for several hours. The baggage compartment is always the hottest during this period.

6. Don't take your pet to the freight area until about a half-hour prior to departure.

7. If you must ship your pet during the dangerous summer months, choose early morning or night flights.

8. If you're traveling overseas, check when veterinary clearance/customs people will be available at the arrival airports. (Ask your airline.) At many airports, such officials are usually not available on weekends or public holidays (and there are many public holidays overseas). Without such clearance, you could have to wait with your pet for many hours in the airport.

9. If possible, schedule international departure and return flights through JFK Airport in New York. The A.S.P.C.A. is very active at this airport and keeps airlines on their toes regarding animal safety. The A.S.P.C.A. also maintains an excellent "animalport" at JFK where you can board dogs and cats overnight.

10. Try to get a confirmed booking from the airline with departure time and routing. Most airlines will give you this confirmation several days in advance. For some reason, TWA and National won't. Pet handlers have reported they usually have to wait until two hours before flight time before getting a definite confirmation from these airlines.

11. If it is a small airport, ask where your animal will be kept until shipment. The Animal Medical Act requires that pets be kept in separate, well-ventilated areas. Temperatures must not go below 45° F. nor rise about 85° F. for more than four hours at a time in this area.

12. You and your vet must decide whether your pet should be tranquilized for the flight. Some vets swear by tranquilizing. Others swear at it. They say it decreases the pet's thirst. Your vet may want to prescribe some medication for motion sickness.

13. After you've picked up the pet from the airline, do not release it in the airport parking lot. Many animals have been so badly frightened by the flight that they may bolt. Postpone your reunion until you're both safely in the car.

14. Watch your pet closely for several weeks after a flight. Noted animal behaviorist Dr. Michael Fox has warned that certain effects of transportation stress may not show up until several weeks after the shipment. These include an increased susceptibility to diseases. If your pet seems unusually sluggish or in pain, take it to a veterinarian.

The ideal kennel

There is considerable difference of opinions about shipping kennels. But most animal authorities would agree on these basic points.

• The airlines usually sell good kennels. These must conform with all of the requirements for sturdiness and ventilation of the Animal Medical Act. The kennel *must* be sturdy to survive occasional whacks from other baggage and still protect the pet inside.

• The kennel should be large enough for the animal to stand up and turn around. (See diagram: How to determine kennel size.) Important exception: This does not apply to Greyhounds. When Greyhounds are confined and nervous, they could begin a whirling dervish dance—spinning around in the box until they injure themselves or drop exhausted. This is a strange characteristic of the Greyhound manifested by no other breed.

• Some pet handlers strongly recommend that you avoid wood, aluminum, and fiberboard kennels. Wood and fiberboard may be chewed. The aluminum may become too cold in winter and too warm in summer. Reinforced plastic seems to be the ideal kennel material. Prices for plastic kennels start at $15.

• Be sure that the kennel has a number of ventilating holes on all sides and the top. The Department of Agriculture requires that at least 8% of each of four sides must be open for ventilation. But this is an absolute minimum. More ventilation is highly desirable. (There is always the possibility that some of the ventilating holes could be blocked by other shipments in the cargo hold or on the loading dock.)

• The kennel must have a strong catch to keep it closed. (You must not lock the kennel. Attendants must be able to get to your pet to water and feed it, particularly if the pet is in a warehouse for 1-2 days.) Recently a very valuable Corgi escaped from a kennel with a weak catch at Dulles International Airport outside of Washington, D.C. The Corgi was finally found on a farm several miles away, sleeping serenely in the chicken coop.

• Line the kennel floor with newspapers or some other absorbent material.

• Put appropriate signs on the kennel which clearly indicate that there is a living creature inside. Use line drawings of the animal if your pet is going overseas where baggage handlers probably won't understand English. Indicate "THIS SIDE UP" with arrows and show your name, address, and phone number where you can be reached. Writer John Richardson suggests adding a human touch—a sign that says, "Please, my name is Red. I need water." This can win some friendly and necessary attention from cargo handlers.

• You may want to consider a kennel which has a small door cut into the larger door. This allows attendants to give your pet food and water without opening the main door and give the pet a chance to run away. Also if your pet snarls or otherwise seems menacing, the attendant may simply splash water through the wire of the larger door. Most of this water goes to waste. Some animal handlers also suggest attaching the water dish to the bottom of the kennel door to prevent the dish from turning over.

A note about costs

Costs vary so widely that it would be impractical to give you many figures.

However, these guidelines may help.

It is usually less expensive to take your pet with you as excess baggage than to ship the pet air cargo. Your pet still travels in its kennel in the cargo hold.

The cost of shipping your pet on international flights is determined by the number of cubic feet the kennel occupies. To ship a West Highland Terrier (in kennel) to Amsterdam from New York would cost you about $32. A Great Dane (in kennel) would cost about $294.

If stopover cities are included in the itinerary, the airline will also bill you for kennel fees overnight. In New York a cat could stay overnight for about $7; in Washington, D.C., $4.25.

How to determine kennel size

First, measure your pet, from the tip of its nose to the root of its tail. See "A" in diagram.

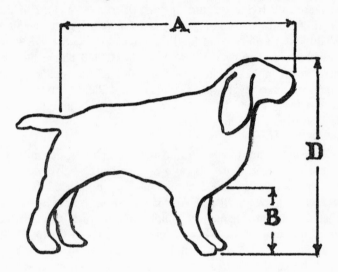

Now measure the height from ground level to elbow joint. See "B" in diagram.

The total number of inches ("A" plus "B") is the correct length of the kennel.

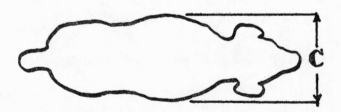

Now measure your pet across the shoulders. See "C".

Multiply this figure by two and you have the width of the kennel.

Now measure the height of your pet standing up. See "D".

The number of inches you get for "D" is the height of the kennel.

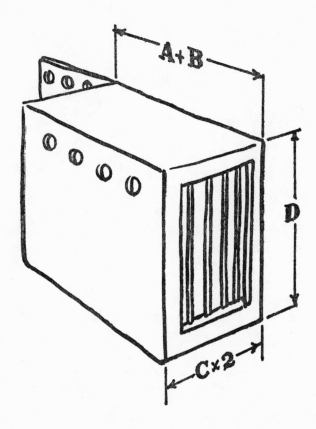

Armed with these figures, you can shop intelligently for the correct size kennel for your pet. Do not exceed these dimensions by more than a few inches or the kennel will be too big or too small for your pet's comfort and safety.

This information is condensed from the McDonnel Douglas Corporation booklet, "Safe Animal Transportation in Passenger Aircraft."

6

HOW TO MAKE YOUR PET A GOOD CAR TRAVELER

Car travel

During a recent ride through the Connecticut countryside, a small brown dog sitting next to the driver was observed doing the following: First it leaped against the driver, causing the car to swerve. It put its front paws on the dashboard and knocked the rear view mirror askew. Then it jumped on the back of the front seat, totally blocking the driver's rear view.

In a car traveling almost sixty miles an hour, these were far more serious than canine pranks. Any one of them could have caused a serious accident. The dog was either too hyperactive to travel in a car or had never been properly trained.

There are some pets which should never be taken in a car. Sick or pregnant animals and puppies head this list, unless you're simply driving them to the vet's. Older pets (over five) may not adjust well to car travel. Some dogs and cats are too nervous to ever become good car travelers. After only a few minutes in a moving car, they become very agitated. They may leap around in the car, salivating profusely and trembling. The ride becomes pure torture for them and everyone in the car. They are dangerous distractions which should be left at home.

But most pets can be trained to become very good car travelers. Some of the nervous nellies simply were introduced to car travel in the wrong way early in their lives. Imagine if you at the age of three were suddenly thrust into a huge machine that shook and roared. After a half hour of continuous noise and bone-rattling stops and starts, you are removed from the machine only to find you have arrived at the dentist's for a tooth extraction.

After a few such experiences you could grow up with a lifelong hatred of automobiles. But the experiences as described are pretty much how many hapless pets are introduced to car travel. After a jolting and bewildering ride in this strange contraption, they are greeted by a vet who stabs them with long needles. Small wonder that some pets head for the closet when they hear the jingle of car keys.

Most dogs and cat experts agree on a *gradual* introduction program to make your pet a good car traveler.

When your pet is still very young, put it in the car parked in your driveway for just a few minutes. Remove your pet immediately if it is about to "scent-post" some new territory in the car. This could cause problems for you later. Dogs can detect one part urine to 60 million parts of water. In case of accident, remove the temptation for your pet to visit the same spot by washing the area several times with soap and water. Then add several drops of an ammonia solution and rub it all over the area.

When your pet becomes a little older, teach it how to get in and out of the car. Toss its favorite toy or a dog biscuit into the car and let your pet retrieve it. Always direct your pet to the back of the car or station wagon. Slap a rolled paper against the leather if your dog or cat climbs into the front seat. Early on your pet should learn that the driver's area is "off limits."

As these sessions increase in length, get into the car with your pet and stay with it for a few minutes. Switch on the car engine, then turn it off. Keep repeating this procedure until your pet becomes accustomed to the noise and vibrations.

If your pet is growing into a large animal, you may want to train it to stay in a carrier in the back seat. All cats should be kept in a carrier. (Cats are very likely to bolt from the car the minute you open the door.) The carrier should be large enough for your pet to turn around in (unless the pet is a Greyhound).

If you're training a dog, be sure it understands the two important commands, "sit" and "stay." Both of these are essential if you are to control your pet when you open the car door in a parking lot or on the road.

If your pet refuses to stay in the back seat, you must then train it to wear a leash or a harness. Secure the end of this leash or harness in the back seat. (Don't loop it over the door handle because your pet's tugging could open the door.) Don't leave the leash or harness on if you leave the animal in the car. The animal could leap over the front seat and strangle itself.

Should you give a hyperactive animal a tranquilizer? The opinion of veterinarians is divided about this. Some say that a tranquilizer makes the pet too woozy, and that a tranquilized cat or dog could tumble around in a moving car and stop drinking water on a hot day (increasing the danger of heatstroke). Others say that a mild tranquilizer can help a pet relax and adjust more easily to car travel. This is a decision you and your veterinarian will have to make together.

If your pet seems to be suffering from motion sickness (symptions: panting, salivating, vomiting), stop the car. Recovery is usually rapid, a few minutes after the motion has stopped. There are motion sickness remedies available which act in the same way as "seasick" pills for humans. They are available in every drug store. But ask your veterinarian about dosage for your pet.

Now that you've come a long way in training your pet to be a good traveler, you can begin to take it on longer rides.

As you're training your pet, you can train yourself in some good habits that will protect your pet.

● Never let a dog stick its head out of the window of a car in motion. Dogs seem to find this pure ecstasy. But grit and dirt can lodge in their eyes and nasal passages.

● *Always* put a reinforced collar on your pet (with your name, address and phone on the plate riveted to the collar). There's always a possibility your pet could run away from the car.

● Do not ride with the windows wide open. Your pet could leap through the window if frightened by a sudden noise or at the sight of another animal. However, the car windows should be open at least two inches. Lack of air is why many dogs, cats (and humans) get carsick.

• Heatstroke is the number one enemy of pets in parked cars. It can kill an animal in the time it takes you to down a hamburger in a roadside restaurant, less than twenty minutes. Cats and dogs, unlike humans, can't get rid of heat through perspiration. They must release excess heat through their lungs as they breathe. Short-nosed breeds, such as Bulldogs, Pekingese, Terriers, and Persian cats are particularly susceptible to heat exhaustion. Heat in a parked car in summer can reach over 120°.

When you pull in to park, always look for the most shady spot. Notice the *length* of the shadow. If you car is just barely inside the shadow, it could be in bright sunlight a few minutes after you've left. Leave the car windows open at least two inches. If you're parked on the street, open the windows two inches on the *street* side. If you open windows on the sidewalk side, children may be tempted to stick fingers at the pet.

• Get your pet out of a parked car as quickly as possible. In addition to the problems of heatstroke, your pet becomes an inviting target for petnappers.

• Travel in the early morning and late afternoon hours, in the spring and fall. You and your pet will both be more comfortable in the cooler temperatures.

• *Never* put your pet in the trunk of a car. The heat and lack of oxygen are killers.

• If your pet is riding in the back of a station wagon or camper with metal floors, check the temperature of the floors. They can get white-hot in summer. You can protect your pet by putting down an old rug.

Preparing for the long trip

Pack your pet's own "suitcase." This can be a box which contains your pet's favorite toy, a blanket, water and food dishes, pet food, a plastic jug filled with water from home, and any essential medications—such as heartworm pills and flea preventatives. Also include the pet's medical papers, a certificate of health signed by your veterinarian, and a current rabies vaccination certificate.

Feed your dog or cat only a light meal the day before the beginning of your trip. Feed only a light snack on the day you start out. If the weather is warm, give your pet plenty of water. It's a good idea to bring water from home rather than pick up water en route. Many animals, like people, are very sensitive to changes in water. On hot days, give your pet ice cubes from the cooler to lick.

Trim your cat's claws. Most cats have four toes with claws on front paws, five toes with claws on back paws. Trim all of them, not closer than ⅛ inch from the veins in the nails. If you don't take this precaution, an irate cat could turn the back of your car into seat-cover slaw.

If you follow the few common-sense precautions described in this chapter, a well-trained pet can make a congenial companion on long car trips. There is even a side benefit. Many driving safety experts say that drivers do not take enough short breaks on long drives to relieve the monotony (and growing inattention to road conditions). Being forced to take your pet for frequent walks is good for both of you.

Some special notes about cats

A metal breadbox with a lid makes a convenient litter box for short trips.

On longer trips, you should take along a regular litter box (disposable ones made especially for traveling cats are a good solution).

If you have a scratching post for your cat, bring it along. This can be a portable gymnasium during car stops.

WHERE TO FIND HOTELS AND MOTELS THAT WELCOME PETS

Hotels & motels for pets

Hotels in Brazil do not have any facilities for pets.

Paula M. Neely, a U.S. diplomat living in Brazil with her husband and a 150-lb. Great Dane, frequently travels all over the countryside. In a recent article in *The New York Times,* she described her technique for getting canine accommodations.

When she, her husband, and the towering Ajax drive up to a hotel, they park their car out of sight. Mrs. Neely then goes to the front desk to request a room. After she has signed in, she tells the reception clerk—almost as an afterthought—that she has a dog.

He smiles and assures her that the hotel welcomes *"cachorrinhos"* (lap dogs).

She then tells him that Ajax could not really be called a little lap dog. But she assures him that her dog is very gentle and likes children and other animals. Then she, her husband, and Ajax go quickly to the room which—by chance—turns out to be her pet's favorite room. It's located directly over the kitchen.

If Mrs. Neely and family were traveling through Europe, the U.S. or Canada, she would not have to go through this well-rehearsed routine to get accommodations for her dog. There are now thousands of hotels and motels that put out the welcome mat for well-behaved cats and dogs. These include major hotel chains such as Hilton, Sheraton, and Quality Inns.

Many hotels and motels do apply certain restrictions. They may require you to keep the pet in its own kennel that you bring with you. Others will admit small dogs only. Some set aside special rooms for dogs, cats, and owners. You may also have to pay a small extra fee. For example, Mr. Dick Combs, owner of the Inn on Lake Waramaug, Conn., charges a fee of $5 (for the whole stay) when a traveler brings along a pet. "This is used to defray the cost of dry-cleaning bedspreads and thoroughly cleaning the room after the pet is gone," said Mr. Combs. "Some guests are allergic to pets and may begin to sneeze if given a room where all traces of the former pet occupant have not been removed.'' Mr. Combs estimates that 10% of his guests now bring their pets. They stay in guest houses outside of the main inn.

Some hotels maintain small kennels, but these may be booked far in advance during peak travel periods. The key to hotel-hopping with your pet is making advance reservations. Always ask if there are any restrictions placed on pets when you make these reservations. In North Carolina it is *against the law* to "permit dogs admittance to any bedroom or rooms used for sleeping purposes in any inn, or hotel.'' The fine: up to $50 or up to 30 days in jail. For you, not Fido. Many North Carolina hotels maintain kennels for dogs because of this law.

You can also camp out with your pets in all National Parks and Forests as long as you keep your pet on a leash or harness. Many commercial campgrounds also permit pets, with some restrictions.

To give you an idea of many far-flung trips you can take with your pet, we've put together some sample U.S. vacations at the end of this chapter. Each sample vacation shows you the hotels, inns and motels along the way which accept pets.

Even many hotels that don't normally take pets can be persuaded if you give them a signed note such as this:

"I have a quiet, well-trained (dog) (cat) that will cause no disturbances or do any damages to furnishings. I will personally be responsible for such furnishings, and as evidence of good faith am attaching a deposit of $20 which you may keep until I check out.''

Vacation manners

Obedience training is an important plus for dogs if you plan to take your friend on vacation. A dog that stands in place when told and does not jump on people (not everyone loves pets) is welcome many places. An animal that runs amuck through a re-

Hotels & motels for pets

sort's prized gardens is unlikely to be a repeat guest, and could run up a sizeable bill for damages.

Keep your pet out of hotel restaurants, cocktail lounges, swimming pools, tennis and beach areas.

Ask the reception clerk where you can walk your pet.

Ask for an outside room, close to the walking area. Avoid walking throughth the lobby if possible. (Many hotels will automatically assign an outside room or a room in their outside motel units when they know you are traveling with a pet.)

Take along the pet's bedding and flea powder. No hotel welcomes fleas.

If your dog has a tendency to bark or tear up the furniture when left alone, you'll have to overcome this bad habit before you check into a hotel. Doctors Peter Borchelt and Daniel Tortora, founders of the Animal Behavior Therapy Clinic in New York, recommended this treatment. Leave your house at the regular time, but return in five minutes. The next day, leave but return within fifteen minutes. You gradually lengthen your absences. This frequently convinces the dog you're liable to pop back in at any minute, and it never really feels it's been deserted and ought to trash the couch.

How to protect your pet

One major problem—your pet may escape when you're away and the maid opens the door to clean the room.

There are several solutions.

You can keep the pet in its own kennel in the room.

Mr. Jim Ball, Marketing Director of the Marriott Twin Bridges Hotel in Alexandria, Va., suggests another way. "Guests with pets should call Housekeeping and ask that the room be made up while the guest is still in the room and can watch the pet. Then after the room is made up, the guest can hang out the "Do not disturb" sign.

If you do have to leave the room unexpectedly, tell the Housekeeping Department that you have a pet in the room and you do not want the door opened.

When you leave the room, turn on the TV set low. This keeps some animals quiet and tends to mask minor noises they might make. It's also a good way to prevent hotel burglaries.

Ask the hotel management about any roach or mouse poisons which may have been used in the room. Have these removed or don't leave your pet in that room.

Put ornamental plants well out of reach of pets. Many such plants are toxic.

Where the welcome mat is out

The following chains which have indicated that they welcome pets include:

Days Inn
Marriott
Sheraton
Hilton
Holiday Inns
Howard Johnson's
Quality Inns
Rodeway Inns
Ramada Inns

Almost all of the above have toll-free numbers (which may change, depending on your location in the country). For the toll-free number for your area, call 800-555-1212.

Even though you know your pet will be welcomed at all of the above chain hotels, it's still a good idea to call specific properties to check if there are restrictions or limitations on pets at that particular hotel. The computer banks maintained by the major hotels (which you can reach with the toll-free phone call) usually can confirm whether or not a hotel accepts pets.

There are also some excellent directories which list thousands of hotels and motor inns.

Good guide books

"Touring with Towser"—a directory of hotels and motels that accommodate guests with dogs. Send $1 per copy to Gaines

Hotels & motels for pets

TWT, P.O. Box 1007, Kankakee, Illinois 60901. Write early. It seems to take this company a long time to respond.

"Mobile Travel Guide"—Seven comprehensive directories which rate lodging, dining and sightseeing, one for each section of the U.S.—"Southwest and South Central Area"—"California and the West"—etc. $4.95 at bookstores. (If the word "Pets" is not specifically included in the hotel listing, they are not welcome.)

"AAA Regional Guidebooks"—These American Automobile Association directories indicate which hotels and motels accept pets. AAA also publishes "Camping and Trailering" which includes restrictions on pets (if any) in public and private campgrounds and trailer parks. All guidebooks are free to AAA members.

"Trailering Parks and Campgrounds"—This annually updated book from the Woodall Publishing Company lists restrictions on pets and indicates where pets are welcome. $5.95 at bookstores.

"Europe's Wonderful Little Hotels and Inns" by Hilary Rubinstein. This 267 page book gives first-hand reviews of three hundred smaller inns and hotels in Europe, from England to Italy. It also provides helpful information for pet owners, such as "dogs not allowed in restaurant" and "pets accommodated on advance arrangement." $9.95 at bookstores. Published by E.P. Dutton.

Eight canine/feline vacations

To give you an idea of just how much freedom you have today in traveling with pets, we've put together eight sample vacations all over the U.S. Each features hotels and motels a typical day's drive apart (250-300 miles) which have indicated they will accept pets. An asterisk by the hotel listing means that some limitations may be placed on pets—such as size. It's essential to call each hotel or motel to check any restrictions on pets as you are making your reservation.

Trip #1: New York City to Maine

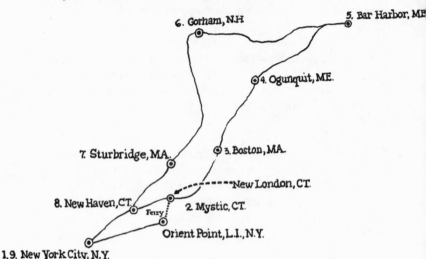

Miles

0   *1. New York City*

      RAMADA INN-MIDTOWN (212) 581-7000
      790 8th Ave. (48th-49th Sts.) Manhattan
      HOLIDAY INN-COLISEUM (212) 581-8100
      440 W. 57th St., Manhattan

120   *2. Mystic, Connecticut*

      via I-95 or ferry from Orient Pt., Long Island to
      New London, CT
      RAMADA INN* (203) 536-4281
      I-95 at CT 27

      Attractions: Mystic seaport, marinelife Aquarium,
      Tail of the Whale Museum (New London), U.S.
      Coast Guard Academy (New London)

217   *3. Boston, Massachusetts*

      CHARLES RIVER (617) 254-0200
      1800 Soldiers Field Rd., Brighton
      2½ mi. NE of Exit 17 I-90

Hotels & motels for pets

HOWARD JOHNSON'S—*KENMORE SQUARE*
(617) 267-3100
U.S. 20 at Commonwealth Ave.
DUNFEY'S PARKER HOUSE (617) 227-8600
60 School St.

334   4. *Ogunquit, Maine*

   MILESTONE MOTOR COURT* (207) 646-2743
   Post Road

      Attractions: Atlantic beach, art galleries, summer
      theatre

510   5. *Bar Harbor—Acadia National Park*

   WONDER VIEW (207) 288-3358
   Eden St.
   ½ mi. N. on ME 3
   or
   camping

689   6. *Gorham, New Hampshire—Mt. Washington, White
   Mt. National Forest*

   TOWN & COUNTRY MOTOR INN (603) 466-3315
   ½ mi. E. on US 2

910   7. *Sturbridge, Massachusetts*

   CARRIAGE HOUSE (617) 347-9000
   MA 131 at US 20

      Attractions: Old Sturbridge Village, Sturbridge
      Auto Museum

994   8. *New Haven, Connecticut*

   RAMADA INN (203) 239-4225
   201 Washington Ave., North Haven
   SHERATON PARK PLAZA* (203) 772-1700
   155 Temple St.
   I-91 Exit 1

1084   9. *New York City*

---

*Some limitations on pets

Trip #2: Philadelphia to Miami

16. Gettysburg, Pa.

1, 17. Philadelphia, Pa.

2. Washington, D.C.

15. Shenandoah National Park

3. Williamsburg, Va.

14. Roanoke, Va.

13. Gatlinburg, Tenn.

4. Fayetteville, N.C.

12. Chattanooga, Tenn.

11. Atlanta, Ga.

5. Charleston, S.C.

10. Valdosta, Ga.

6. Jacksonville, Fla.

7. Orlando, Fla.

9. Tampa, Fla.

8. Miami, Fla.

Miles

0   *1. Philadelphia*

HILTON INN (215) 755-9500
10 St. and Packer Ave.   SW of Whitman Bridge

133   *2. Washington, D.C.*

MARRIOTT TWIN BRIDGES (703) 628-4200
333 Jefferson Davis Highway, Arlington, VA
I-95 and US 1. Request room in motel unit.
HOLIDAY INN- CONNECTICUT AVE. (202)
332-9300
1900 Connecticut Ave., N.W.

Hotels & motels for pets

288   *3. Williamsburg, VA*

BEST WESTERN PATRICK HENRY INN
(804) 229-9540
2 blocks E of Colonial Capitol Bldg. on US 60
NOTE: "Old Country," Busch's theme park, has
   kennel facilities for visitors

502   *4. Fayetteville, NC*

HOLIDAY INN (919) 483-0332
7 blocks S. on US 301 bypass
Kennel

705   *5. Charleston, SC*

BEST WESTERN KING CHARLES INN
(803) 723-7451
237 Meeting St.

958   *6. Jacksonville, FL*

HILTON HOTEL (904) 398-3561
565 S. Main St.
DAYS INN (904) 757-5000
Airport Rd. at I-95

1103   *7. Orlando, FL*

CONTEMPORARY RESORT (305) 824-8000
on Disney World grounds
Kennel
DAYS INN (305) 628-2727
I-4 Lee Rd. exit
NOTE: Disney World and Kennedy Space Center
   have kennel vacilities for visitors.

1400   *8. Miami, FL*

MARDI GRAS (305) 573-7700
3400 Biscayne Blvd. 1 block S. of I-195

1668   *9. Tampa, FL*

HOLIDAY INN APOLLO BEACH (813) 645-3271
20 mi. S, 2 mi. W of US 41
Surfside Rd., Apollo Beach

1893   *10. Valdosta, GA*

     DAVIS BROS. QUALITY INN NORTH
     (912) 244-8610
     I-5 at GA 94

2114   *11. Atlanta, GA*

     HOLIDAY INN—SIX FLAGS WEST
     (404) 691-4100
     4225 Fulton Industrial Blvd
     1½ mi. W of I-285

2228   *12. Chattanooga, TN*

     SHERATON—DOWNTOWN (615) 756-5150
     407 Chestnut St. at 4 St.
     I-124 exit at 4 St.

2373   *13. Gatlinburg, TN—Great Smoky Mtns. National Park*

     HOWARD JOHNSON'S (615) 436-5621
     Parkway, 1 block N on US 441

2610   *14. Roanoke, VA*

     HOLIDAY INN—CIVIC CENTER (703) 342-8961
     Williamson Rd. at Orange Ave.
     South of I-581 Orange Ave. exit
     Kennel

2750   *15. Shenandoah National Park, VA via Skyline Drive*

     Camping or
     BIG MEADOWS LODGE* (703) 999-2221
     Skyline Drive 19 mi. S at Thornton Gap Entrance
     from US 211

2906   *16. Gettysburg, PA–Gettysburg Nat. Military Park*

     HOWARD JOHNSON'S (717) 334-1188
     301 Steinwehr Ave.
     1 mi. S on US 15 Business

3014   *17. Philadelphia*

———

*Some limitations on pets

Trip #3: Chicago to Minneapolis

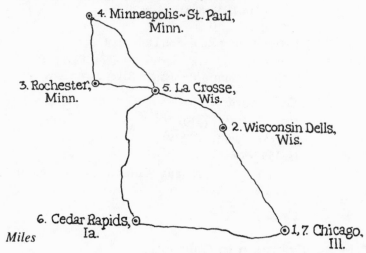

Miles

0   *1. Chicago*

    RODEWAY INN (312) 693-5800
    6515 N. Cumberland Ave.
    HOLIDAY INN (312) 943-9200
    644 N. Lake Shore Dr.
    Kennel

196   *2. Wisconsin Dells, WI*

    RAINBOW MOTEL (608) 254-7606
    612 Vine St.
    1½ blocks S. off Broadway
       Attractions: The Dells, Circus World Museum at
       Baraboo

342   *3. Rochester, MN*

    HOLIDAY INN—DOWNTOWN (508) 288-3231
    220 S. Broadway on US 63

427   *4. Minneapolis-St. Paul, MN*

    HOLIDAY INN—AIRPORT #1 (612) 854-4000
    7800 34th Ave. South Bloomington
    S of I-494, 34th Ave. exit

571   *5. LaCrosse, WI*

RAMADA INN (608) 785-0420
2325 Bainbridge St.
I-90 at Airport Rd.—French Is. exit

Attractions: Oktoberfest, Great River Road,
Grandad Bluff, Mississippi River excursions

745   *6. Cedar Rapids, IA*

HOLIDAY INN (319) 365-9441
2500 William Blvd. SW
IA 149 N of US 30

Attractions: Amana Colonies, Art Center,
Palisades-Kepler Park

986   *7. Chicago*

Trip #4: Colorado to California

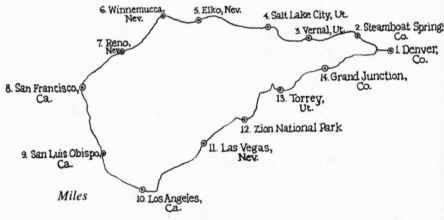

0   *1. Denver*

RADISSON DENVER HOTEL (303) 861-2000
1790 Grant St.

166   *2. Steamboat Springs, CO*

HOLIDAY INN (303) 879-2250
3 mi. E on US 40
Kennel

Hotels & motels for pets

331 *3. Vernal, UT*

DINOSAUR MOTEL (801) 789-2660
251 E. Main St.

> *Attractions:* Dinosaur National Monument,
> Flaming Gorge Dam and National Recreation Area

507 *4. Salt Lake City, UT*

TRAVELODGE AT SIXTH SOUTH
(801) 521-7373
161 W. 6 South St.

783 *5. Elko, NV*

HOLIDAY INN (702) 738-8425
1 mi. E. on US 40
Kennel

TOPPER'S (702) 738-7245
9 blocks E. on US 40

> *Attractions:* casinos, museum, National Basque
> Festival

863 *6. Winnemucca, NV*

MOTEL 6* (702) 623-5775
1 mi. W on US 40

WINNERS INN* (702) 623-2511
Winnemucca Blvd at Lay

1030 *7. Reno, NV*

HARRAH'S (702) 786-3232
210 N. Center St.
Kennel

MOTEL 6* (702) 0180
866 N. Wells Ave.
½ block S. of I-80 Wells Ave. exit

1259 *8. San Francisco, CA*

HOLIDAY INN—GOLDEN GATEWAY
(415) 441-4000
1500 Van Ness Ave. at California St.

1490   *9. San Luis Obispo, CA*

> BEST WESTERN OLIVE TREE INN
> (805) 544-2800
> 1100 Olive St.
> 1 block W. of Morro Bay or Santa Rosa St. exits US
> 101   *Attractions:* Mission, museum, Mozart Festival

1673   *10. Los Angeles, CA*

> BEST WESTERN EXECUTIVE MOTOR INN
> (213) 380-6910
> 457 S. Mariposa Ave.
> Hollywood Freeway Vermont exit
> UNIVERSITY HILTON (213) 748-4141
> 3545 S. Figueroa St.
> 3 mi. S of CA 11 Exposition exit

1955   *11. Las Vegas, NV*

> HOLIDAY INN—CENTER STRIP (702) 732-2333
> 3475 Las Vegas Blvd. South
> MOTEL 6 (702) 736-4904
> 195 E. Tropicana Blvd.   I-15 Tropicana exit

2122   *12. Zion National Park, UT*

> Camping* (pets must be kept on leash)
> TERRACE BROOK LODGE (801) 772-3932
> 1½ mi. S of S park entrance on UT 15

2309   *13. Torrey, UT—Capitol Reef National Park*

> Camping* (pets must be kept on leash)
> RIM ROCK MOTEL (801) 425-3843
> 8 mi W of Park Visitor Center on UT 24

2512   *14. Grand Junction, CO*–Colorado National
Monument

> BEST WESTERN SANDMAN (303) 243-4150
> 708 Horizon Dr.   at I-70 Airport exit

2769   *15. Denver*

---

*Some limitations on pets

Trip #5: California

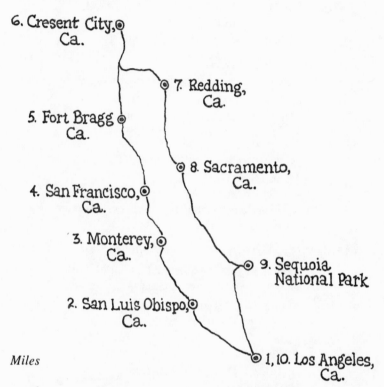

6. Cresent City, Ca.

7. Redding, Ca.

5. Fort Bragg Ca.

8. Sacramento, Ca.

4. San Francisco, Ca.

3. Monterey, Ca.

9. Sequoia National Park

2. San Luis Obispo, Ca.

1, 10. Los Angeles, Ca.

Miles

0   *1. Los Angeles*

BEST WESTERN EXECUTIVE MOTOR INN
(213) 380-6910
457 S. Mariposa Ave.
Hollywood Freeway Vermont exit
UNIVERSITY HILTON (243) 748-4141
3545 S. Figueroa St.
3 mi. S of CA 11 Exposition exit

183   *2. San Luis Obispo*

BEST WESTERN OLIVE TREE INN (805) 544-2800
1000 Olive St.
1 block W of US 101 Santa Rosa St. exit

320　　*3. Monterey*

　　　HILTON INN RESORT (408) 373-6141
　　　1000 Aguajito Rd.
　　　1 block E. of CA 1 Aguajito exit

435　　*4. San Francisco*

　　　HOLIDAY INN—GOLDEN GATEWAY
　　　(415) 441-4000
　　　1500 Van Ness Ave. at California St.

601　　*5. Fort Bragg*

　　　PINE BEACH INN (707) 964-5603
　　　4½ mi. S on CA 1
　　　Pets $1 extra charge
　　　　Attractions: Botancial Gardens, Museum, Rail-
　　　　road, State Parks

615　　*6. Crescent City—Redmond National Park*

　　　Camping* (pet must be kept on leash)
　　　TOWN HOUSE (707) 464-4176
　　　444 Redwood Highway
　　　½ mi. S on US 101

836　　*7. Redding*

　　　HOLIDAY INN (916) 246-1500
　　　1900 Hilltop Dr.
　　　I-5 Hilltop Dr. exit
　　　MOTEL 6 (916) 243-8700
　　　1640 Hilltop Dr.
　　　I-5 Hilltop Dr. exit
　　　　Attractions: Lassen Volcanic Nat. Park, Whis-
　　　　keytown-Shasta-Trinity Nat. Recreation Area

998　　*8. Sacramento*

　　　WOODLAKE INN (916) 922-6251
　　　500 Leisure Lane
　　　Off CA 160 at Canterbury Rd.

1233　*9. Three Rivers—Sequoia and Kings Canyon National
　　　Parks*

Hotels & motels for pets

Camping* (pet must be kept on leash)
GRANT GROVE LODGE (209) 335-2314
Kings Canyon Nat. Park
BEST WESTERN HOLIDAY LODGE
(209) 561-4119
8 mi. W of Sequoia Nat. Park entrance on CA 198

1445   *10. Los Angeles*

Trip #6: Washington to Oregon

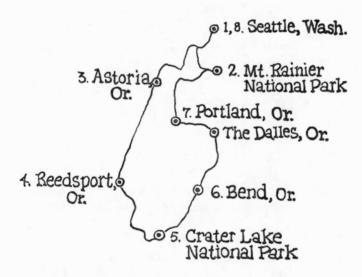

Miles

0   *1. Seattle*

     HOLIDAY INN—SOUTH (206) 762-0300
     11244 Pacific Highway South
     9 mi. S. on WA 99
     Kennel

---

*Some limitations on pets

SEA-TAC RED LION INN (206) 246-8600
18740 Pacific Highway South, at 188 St.
13 mi. S. on WA 99
Near Seattle-Tacoma International Airport
RAMADA INN (206) 365-0700
2140 N. Northgate Way
5 mi. N. I-5 at 110 St.

95　　2. *Mt. Rainier National Park*

Camping* (pet must be kept on leash)
REST-A-SPELL (206) 569-2355
5 mi. E. of Ashford on WA 706

254　　3. *Astoria, Oregon*

THUNDERBIRD (503) 325-7373
400 Industry St.
1 block N. of US 30, 1 block W. of Columbia River Bridge

454　　4. *Reedsport, Oregon*

TROPICANA* (503) 271-3671
½ mi. S. on US 101
VILLA WEST (503) 997-3457
on US 101 20 mi. N. in Florence, OR
Attractions: Oregon Dunes National Recreation Area, Scenic Drive on US 101 from Astoria

656　　5. *Crater Lake National Park*

Camping* (pets must be kept on leash)
CRATER LAKE LODGE* (503) 594-2511
on S. side Crater Lake
Pets in cabins

765　　6. *Bend, Oregon*

RED LION (503) 382-83-84
849 N.E. 3 St.
½ mi. E. on US 97
Attractions: Newberry Crater, ski area, several state parks, scenery

Hotels & motels for pets

976   7. *Portland, via The Dalles*

    The Dalles

    PORTAGE INN (503) 298-5502
    3223 N.E. Frontage Rd.
    ½ block E. of US 197

    Attractions: Dam, locks

    Portland

    BEST WESTERN KING'S WAY INN
    (503) 233-6331
    420 N.E. Holladay St.
    3 blocks E. of I-5

    IMPERIAL HOTEL (503) 228-7221
    400 S.W. Broadway at Stark St.

      Attractions: College, Oregon Museum of Science and Industry, American Rhododendron Soc. Garden

1154   8. *Seattle*

Trip #7: Dallas to Chicago to New Orleans

Miles

0   *1. Dallas, TX*

    LA QUINTA (214) 252-6546
    4105 W. Airport Freeway, Irving
    TX 183 at Esters Rd.

    LE BARON (214) 634-8550
    1055 Regal Row
    TX 183, 3 blocks S. of I-35E

206   *2. Oklahoma City, OK*

    HILTON INN WEST (405) 947-7681
    401 S. Meridian Ave.

---

*Some limitations on pets

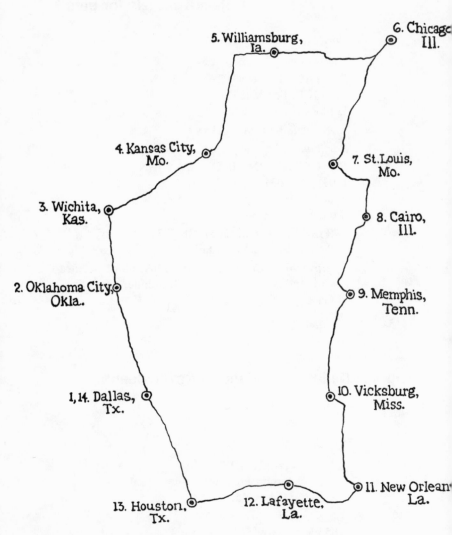

1. Dallas, Tx.
2. Oklahoma City, Okla.
3. Wichita, Kas.
4. Kansas City, Mo.
5. Williamsburg, Ia.
6. Chicago, Ill.
7. St. Louis, Mo.
8. Cairo, Ill.
9. Memphis, Tenn.
10. Vicksburg, Miss.
11. New Orleans, La.
12. Lafayette, La.
13. Houston, Tx.
14. Dallas, Tx.

I-40 Meridian Ave. exit
HOLIDAY INN—CENTRAL (405) 232-2241
520 W. Main St.
Kennel

365   *3. Wichita, KS*

HOLIDAY INN-MIDTOWN (316) 267-6211
1000 N. Broadway

Hotels & motels for pets

562 *4. Kansas City, MO*

RAMADA STADIUM INN (816) 861-5600
5100 E. Linwood Blvd
3 blocks SW of I-70 Van Brunt exit

844 *5. Williamsburg, IA*

WILLIAMSBURG TRAVELODGE (319) 668-1522
1 mi. N. on Iowa 149—S. of I 80
Attractions: Amana Colonies

1097 *6. Chicago, IL*

RODEWAY INN (312) 693-5800
5615 N. Cumberland Ave.

HOLIDAY INN (312) 943-9200
644 N. Lake Shore Dr.
Kennel

1386 *7. St. Louis, MO*

HOLIDAY INN-DOWNTOWN (314) 231-3232
2211 Market St.
on US 40 Business Loop
Kennel

1533 *8. Cairo, IL*

MORSE MOTEL (618) 734-2820
307 Washington Ave.
on US 51

   Attractions: Magnolia Manor, Magnolia Festival,
   Ft. Defiance State Park

1695 *9. Memphis, TN*

BEST WESTERN RIVER BLUFF INN
(901) 948-9005
340 W. Illinois Ave.
I-55 exit 12C

HOLIDAY INN-CENTRAL (901) 278-4100
1837 Union Ave. at McLean
on US 64, 70, 72, 79
Kennel

1921   *10. Vicksburg, MS*
        HOLIDAY INN (601) 636-4551
        US 80 at I-20
        Kennel
          Attractions: Vicksburg National Military Park and
          Cemetery

2135   *11. New Orleans, LA*
        VIEUX CARRE MOTOR LODGE (504) 524-0461
        920 N. Ramport St.
        la French Quarter
        Kennel

2300   *12. Lafayette, LA via US 90*
        HOLIDAY INN - SOUTH (318) 234-8521
        3 mi. SE on US 90
        Kennel

2517   *13. Houston, TX*
        HOLIDAY INN-MEDICAL CENTER
        (713) 797-1110
        6701 S. Main St.
        Kennel

2760   *14. Dallas, TX*

Trip #8: New York City to Toronto

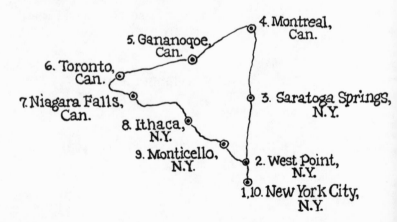

Hotels & motels for pets

Miles

0   *1. New York City*

RAMADA INN-MIDTOWN (212) 581-7000
790 8th Ave.
between 48th - 49th Streets
HOLIDAY INN-COLISEUM (212) 581-8100
440 W. 57th St.

50   *2. Highland Falls, NY—West Point*

PALISADE* (914) 446-9400
on US 218 off US 9W

178   *3. Saratoga Springs, NY*

GATEWAY MOTEL (518) 584-2611
260 Maple Ave.
HOLIDAY INN (518) 584-4550
Broadway and Circular Sts.
Kennel

374   *4. Montreal, Quebec, Canada*

HOLIDAY INN-DOWNTOWN (514) 842-6111
420 Sherbrooke St.
Kennel

521   *5. Gananoque, Ontario, Canada*

St. Lawrence Islands National Park (U.S.A.)
COUNTRY SQUIRE (613) 382-3511
715 King St. East
½ mi. W. of 401 exit 107

697   *6. Toronto, Ontario, Canada*

HYATT REGENCY (416) 964-6511
21 Avenue Rd. at Bloor St.
HOLIDAY INN EAST (416) 293-8171
22 Metropolitan Rd., Scarborough
Kennel

NOTE: There is an animal park at the Metro Toronto Zoo where you can leave your pet.

767 7. *Niagara Falls, Ontario, Canada*

CLIFFSIDE MOTEL (416) 356-5620
4886 Clifton Hill
1 block W. of falls off ONT 20

936 8. *Ithaca, NY*

MEADOW COURT (607) 273-3885
529 S. Meadow St.
on NY 13
HOLIDAY INN (607) 257-3100
310 N. Triphammer Rd.
off NY 13

1089 9. *Monticello, NY*

HOLIDAY MOUNTAIN MOTOR LODGE
(914) 796-3000
Exit 109 NY 17

Attractions: Catskill resort region, Catskill Park

1189 10. *New York City*

Remember when you're out driving that a number of amusement areas now offer kennels where visitors can board their pets for the day. For example, Disneyland in California operates the "Disneyland Kennel Club." For 50¢ the Club will watch your pet and even feed it. Disney World in Florida offers similar facilities. So do theme parks such as Marriott's Great America in Gurnee, Illinois, and Santa Clara, California. Busch Garden's Old Country in Williamsburg, Virginia, and Magic Mountain in California will also look after your pet while you enjoy yourself. Six Flags in Atlanta, Georgia, has a "Park-a-pet" service for $1. Before you leave your pet in a hot car, always ask at the entrance to the amusement area about kenneling facilities.

---

*Some limitations on pets

Before leaving your pets alone in a hotel room, check that there are no insecticides or other poisons around. Remember that some ornamental plants used in hotel rooms are poisonous.

8

EMERGENCIES!
HOW TO
HELP A SICK
OR HURT FRIEND

Emergencies

Emergencies or sudden illnesses can strike your pet at any time. But when your pet is afflicted while you're traveling with it hundreds of miles from home, you may have a particular feeling of helplessness.

There are several common mistakes that many travelers make under these circumstances.

Because they don't know how or where to reach a veterinarian, they may try to nurse their pet back to health on their own. That may work with minor illnesses, but with many animal health problems prolonged delays before getting professional treatment can have serious consequences for the pet. Heatstroke, for example, is a common problem that requires prompt professional help to save the pet's life.

If you're traveling in the U.S., consult the veterinarian notices in the Yellow Pages. Many list hours and specialties. In some areas veterinarian associations provide 24-hour-a-day referral services. You can also call a local animal hospital which almost always has a veterinarian on call. (Incidentally the frequent note you'll see in vets' notices—"treats small animals only"— doesn't mean the vets won't treat your Great Dane. It means the vets specialize in dogs, cats and domestic pets rather than farm animals.)

If you're traveling overseas, call the nearest U.S. embassy or consulate and request a list of English-speaking veterinarians.

Another mistake some travelers make is to give their pets medications designed for humans. The dog develops a cough; the owner doctors it with cough syrup. But this syrup may have ingredients which are dangerous for dogs. Another traveler may give his animal an aspirin. But aspirin can have dangerous side effects on some animals, particularly cats.

Rule of thumb: never give your pet *any* medication unless it has been prescribed by a veterinarian.

Another mistake that owners sometimes make in emergencies is to get too close to an injured pet without taking precautions. The pet is frightened and may be suffering shock. In a panic it may bite or claw *anybody* who comes too close. If the animal is snapping, muzzle it with a heavy cord looped around the dog's nose just in back of the nose. Tie it under the chin.* If you are having trouble getting close to the animal, keep a jacket rolled around your arm and use it as a buffer to ward of bites.

It's important to keep your head. This is hard because you know a pet that you love is in pain. Drive to the vet's quickly but don't speed. An injured owner is no help to himself or his pet.

Keep this book with you when you travel. Turn to this chapter if you run into a problem. The *Problem* and *First Aid* are printed in bold type for quick reference. But these suggestions, culled from professional veterinarian sources, should never replace the veterinarian. They can help your pet until you get your dog or cat to a veterinarian or animal hospital.

Problem: bites, open wounds

When you travel across the country with your pet, you will encounter many different kinds of animals—not all of whom will like you or your pet. While much of the fighting between pets is ritual with much more growling and hissing than fighting, animals can and do inflict serious bites on each other. Even though a bite may leave only a small puncture wound on the skin surface with little external bleeding, there could be internal bleeding and severed muscles.

First aid

Use plenty of soap and water to cleanse the open wound. If there is extensive bleeding, clamp a clean handkerchief over the wound and apply pressure. This usually stops the flow of blood and encourages clotting. If the bleeding is excessive, you may want to apply a tourniquet *if* you've had first aid training in the use of tourniquets. (Many people don't know how to use tourniquets and do more harm than good.) Get your pet to the vet promptly.

Special note about rabies

Because of the widespread availability of vaccinations and stiff public health requirements, the incidence of rabies in cats and dogs has been greatly reduced. However, if your pet is bitten by a strange animal, you should try to track down the owner by asking people in the neighborhood. Report the incident

* Do not use a muzzle if the animal is having a seizure.

to the police. If the animal in question is behaving strangely, the police may require that it be confined for ten days to be sure the animal is not infected with rabies. Your pet is protected by the rabies vaccine *if* the vaccine is current.

Wild animals are much more likely to carry rabies. In recent years there have been rabies scares in some of the National Parks. In the spring of 1978 a squirrel suspected of being rabid attacked several people and animals in the heart of St. Louis. If a wild animal attacks your pet, attempt to kill the animal (without being bitten yourself!) and take the body to the vet for rabies examination. *Always* report such incidents to local authorities. You could be doing other people in the area a big favor.

Problem: broken bones

What if you were camping with your pet and it suddenly tumbled off the rocks? You suspect broken bones.

First aid

Before you attempt to treat your pet, always muzzle it (see above). Your pet will be in considerable pain and will probably be snapping. You want to keep the fracture as immobile as possible to avoid further injury. Safest way to transport the injured animal is in a cardboard box. To avoid lifting the animal and possibly causing more injury, you can follow this procedure. Cut the edges of the box on one side and lower the flap. Slide the animal into the box as carefully as possible. Then seal the flap back in place with tape. When you carry this box, try to keep a pillow or a rolled up peice of clothing between you and the box to prevent the pet from biting you. Get your pet to the veterinarian promptly.

Problem: car accidents

Unfortunately car accidents are always a potential hazard when you travel. Your pet could leap through a car window into the road and be injured by the fall or struck by another car. An unleashed animal in a rest area could dash onto the highway. That old saw about prevention being the best medicine is still true. You should keep windows rolled down only a few inches when you drive. You should not let your pet roam free when you stop the car. But if the worst does occur despite your precautions, there are immediate actions you should take.

First aid

You must get the pet off the road as quickly as possible. Both you and the pet could be struck by another car. If you have a blanket or piece of carboard in the car, slide your pet on to this. Then gently slide your pet off the road. Be very careful not to get too close to your pet's head because of the danger of biting. One usually safe method is to grab the animal from behind, at the loose fold of skin around the neck and over the hip. Slide the animal backfirst on to the blanket.

Stop any excessive bleeding by applying pressure to the wound with a clean handkerchief or bandage. Keep the pet as warm as possible while transporting it to the vet.

If your pet has stopped breathing, it is possible to administer the canine/feline equivalent of mouth-to-mouth resuscitation. Cup your hands firmly around your pet's nose, closing its mouth. Breath into your pet's nose for three seconds. Then relax for two seconds. Repeat. Keep this procedure going until your pet is breathing normally again.

Problem: convulsions

A few years back people would say the dog was having a "fit." Now it's called a convulsion. But whatever the word, it is a frightening experience for the pet and the pet owner. The dog or cat may become unconscious, lying on its back and kicking its legs wildly. Usually the animal will also salivate profusely. The convulsion usually is brief, most lasting about a minute. A convulsion may have many possible causes such as poisoning, severe head injuries or some infectious disease.

First aid

Stay out of the pet's way during the seizure. Cats particularly may show signs of rage. *Do not* follow the old remedy of trying to put something between the pet's teeth. Do not attempt to muzzle the animal. You can confine the animal and restrict its movements by putting a blanket around it. Remember that the animal will be very dazed when coming out of a seizure and could fall down a stairs and injure itself further. Watch your pet closely. If breathing stops, give artificial respiration (mouth-to-nose) as described in CAR ACCIDENTS above. If the seizure lasts more than 5 minutes, get to the vet immediately.

Problem: diarrhea/vomiting

Many pets will react to sudden changes in diet or activities by showing symptoms of diarrhea and stomach upset. That means traveling pets are prime candidates for these problems!

First aid

If the diarrhea continues, give your pet water but no food. Your veterinarian can prescribe the medicine to arrest the diarrhea. Food and water should be withheld in the case of continuous vomiting, until you've seen the veterinarian.

Problem: heatstroke

An all too typical situation in summer months: the pet owner returns to his car parked in the sun to find his pet panting and unconscious in the backseat, a victim of heatstroke. The skin will be hot and dry to the touch.

First aid

You have to remove the pet from the hot area *immediately*. Try to reduce its body temperature as quickly as possible. You can soak rags in cold water and put over the pet's body. Or hose the pet down with cold water. If your pet has stopped breathing, give artificial respiration. Have a friend fan the pet as you take it to the vet as quickly as possible. Heatstroke can be a very serious problem.

Special note

No nose is bad news. Short-nosed animals such as Bulldogs, Terriers and Persian cats are particularly vulnerable to heatstroke because they sometimes can't cool themselves effectively by breathing. Never muzzle a dog or cat and leave it in a hot environment.)

Problem: poisoning

Dogs and cats can be extremely inquisitive. That's a lovable trait, but it sometimes gets them into a lot of trouble. A dog that nibbles a garden treated with insecticide could become very ill, very quickly. A cat in a hotel room may want to sample one of the ornamental plants, many of which are poisonous. Even some apparently harmless substances that you pack in your suitcase could poison a pet. For example, a cat left alone in a tent could walk through some spilled sun tan lotion. Being a born licker, it would probably cleanse itself by licking off the lotion. But ingredients in some sun tan lotions can be harmful to pets.

First aid

Call the veterinarian immediately for advice. Tell the vet what kind of poison you think your pet may have swallowed. When some poisons are ingested (such as acids or petroleum products), the vet will probably ask to see the animal immediately. With other poisons which are not corrosive, the vet may ask you to induce the pet to vomit. If you do not know the specific poison and are in a wilderness situation, you can at least dilute the poison by giving the pet water or milk. If you're in a small town anywere near a drug store, mix the milk or water with activated charcoal. When transporting a poisoned pet to an animal hospital, keep the head lower than the rest of the body so that fluids can drain out.

Problem: shock

Shock may accompany any serious illness or injury. Usually the animal begins to shiver violently. There will be rapid breathing and heartbeat. The animal may become very sluggish in its movements, with a subnormal body temperature (below 101.5 degrees).

First aid

Keep the pet as warm as possible. Keep the head level with the rest of the body and gently massage the pet's legs to improve circulation. Caution: Do not use a heating pad or lamp. Because of the pet's poor circulation, it can easily be burned. The most effective treatment of severe shock is the injection of intravenous fluids, and this can only be done at a veterinarian's office or an animal hospital. Get professional medical advice quickly, a suggestion we can't overemphasize.

Special warning about heartworms

Canine heartworms are carried by mosquitoes. Once bitten by a mosquito, the dog becomes host for long (up to 14 inch) heartworms which settle in the heart. This disease which shows few symptoms until late stages when it may become fatal has now spread through much of the U.S. and many parts of Canada.

Travelers going into new area, particularly during the summer mosquito months, should certainly get heartworm pills from their veterinarian. These pills, taken daily, can kill the worm larvae in the blood. Caution: do not take heartworm pills from a friend without having your pet tested first to be sure it is free of heartworms. The medication could harm infected pets.

Here is partial list of some common plants, items and products a traveling pet could come in contact with. All can be hazardous.

- Most photographic chemicals
- Antifreeze
- Gasoline
- Kerosine
- Drain cleaners
- Lead paint
- Slug and snail bait
- Pine oil
- Many household cleaners, polishes, disinfectants
- Bath oils
- Perfumes
- Diet pills
- Many deodorants
- Laxatives
- Nail polish
- Shaving lotion
- Many sun tan lotions
- Many shampoos
- Insecticides

Puppies are particularly vulnerable because they eat anything in sight. Older animals usually are more discriminating, but any pet could come in contact with spilled substances.

9

HOW TO DOUBLE
YOUR CHANCES OF
FINDING A LOST PET

Finding a lost pet

On a hot July day in the summer of 1977, Mr. Paul Mergard of Brewster, N.Y. set out for a trip to Florida in a VW bus. He was accompanied by a beautiful 13-year-old Collie named Candy. Near Scranton, Pa., he stopped for gas and asked the attendant to wipe his windows. The attendant rolled down the rear window and left it open.

Mr. Mergard did not notice the open window when he returned to the bus. He drove down a long winding road and reduced his speed to under ten miles an hour. When he stopped the bus and turned around to speak to Candy, he was horrified to find that his collie had disappeared.

He immediatly retraced his route looking for Candy. For ten terrible days he cruised that road and the area looking for his dog, but there was no trace. He drove on to Florida, convinced that Candy had been killed or was lost for good.

Unfortunately, variations of this scenario are repeated hundreds of times each year all over the country. Said a spokeswoman for the Los Angeles ASPCA, "Our major problem involves lost dogs. We get calls from our shelters saying, 'We have a lost dog here with a Florida collar,' or 'We have a cat here from Michigan.' People who travel think that their animals won't get away. But they're bringing their pets into a totally new environment. When the pets get lost, they're disoriented and can't find their way back to their owners."

But the true story of Candy has a happy ending. Some days after Mr. Mergard's trip, Mr. and Mrs. Silvette of Wilkes-Barre, Pa., saw a starved, bedraggled Collie limping along a dirt road. They took the dog home with them and fed it. While they were cleaning the Collie, they noticed a number tattooed on the dog's inside flank. The Silvettes called the National Dog Registry (NDR) in Carmel, N.Y., and reported they had found a "registered" Collie. The NDR searched their files of owner Social Security numbers, and found that the numbered dog belonged to Mr. Mergard. After a number of long-distance calls, they finally located Mr. Mergard in Florida who joyfully flew back to Pennsylvania for an unexpected reunion with Candy.

But not all lost pet stories end so pleasantly. Some experts estimate that only about 15% of all lost pets are ever returned to their original owners. What can you do if your pet is lost when you're on a trip or missing from your backyard?

Don't panic. There are six steps you can take which can more than double your chances of getting your pet back. But more about these shortly.

First, let's look at the most common reasons pets disappear from the home and on the road, and what you can do to prevent their loss.

• Many dogs and cats wander off from gasoline stations and roadside rest areas. Some, like Candy, leap through an open car window. Other unleashed pets take off after other animals. After the chase, they can't find their way back. You should always keep your dog on a leash and your cat on a harness when you reach a rest area. If your cat won't abide a harness, keep it in the car with a kitty litter container. Open car windows only about two inches, wide enough for absolutely essential ventilation. But not wide enough to become an escape hatch.

• Many pet owners who move to country homes or rural summer places now believe their dog or cat has the "right" to roam free. This is a cruel freedom. Many free-roaming animals are hit by cars. Others who have not "scent-posted" trees and other objects around a new house to mark the bounds of their territory may wander off and get lost.

You should not let your pet run free. It is not a kindness. Keep them in a secure, fenced backyard. If you tether your dog, don't trust to ropes, which frequently break. Use a smooth linked chain. Shout "Bad Dog" if you ever find your escape artist burrowing under a fence, and slap a roll of paper on the ground near the pet. Or fill an empty beer can with pebbles and throw it on the ground. Repeat until your pet learns that tunneling under the fence seems to cause some very bad, noisy things to happen.

• Your dog or cat could be petnapped. "Petnapping is a most urgent problem, and it's growing," said Ms. Fay Brisk, a consumer activist who has been very involved in protecting the rights and well-being of pets. "You'd be amazed at the number of people who believe that petnapping can't happen to them. I just had a call from a woman who had a miniature Greyhound. She tied it outside of a library for only a few minutes while she returned a book. When she got back, she discovered that some-one had stolen her dog."

Finding a lost pet

There are no accurate statistics about the incidence of petnapping. Police and local human societies seldom keep track. Many pets were originally stolen for research laboratories. Then stiff laws were passed by Congress which regulated the sale of animals to laboratories. This eliminated much of the incentive for petnapping. But now dognapping in particular seems to be making a comeback, for new reasons. Many healthy young dogs are stolen and sold to "puppy mills" for breeding purposes or to trainers of guard dogs. The demand for trained guard dogs in the U.S. seems insatiable, and some now command prices up to $1500. For this reason, the most popular target breed of petnappers looking for possible guard dog candidates is the Doberman Pinscher, followed by the German Shepherd. The breed most stolen for laboratory use is the Beagle. Purebreds are usually the most common petnapping victims, but no pet is really completely safe. Hunting dogs, especially during the hunting season, are often stolen.

Nor is any part of the country immune. The tiny town of New Paltz, N.Y. (population 6,000) was recently blitzed by dognappers. So were parts of Northern Viriginia and Ohio.

Some authorities who have been following the growth of petnapping describe the typical operation like this. Much of the organized dognapping rings in the East seem to originate in New Jersey. Individual thieves usually are known as a "dog jockey" or "buncher." The "dog jockey" may cruise a suburban neighborhood in a panel truck, looking especially for young purebred dogs on the loose. He may keep a bitch in heat in the back of the truck to lure the roaming animal inside. After capturing a truckload of animals, he will drive to some central "bunching" place. This is usually a farm or isolated house in the suburbs, with a number of "no trespassing" signs.

The dogs are then sorted for possible sale. Some animals are sent to Pennsylvania where most of the kennels which sell to laboratories are concentrated. Others are sold to a few guard dog trainers who do not ask a lot of questions. Still others become breeding stock for "puppy mills." The petnappers are avid readers of Lost & Found columns. If the owner seems to be offering a large reward (and $100 to $500 is not an uncommon offer by a heartbroken pet owner), the thief will call and report the animal has been "found" and claim the reward.

On city streets petnapping is usually less organized. The thieves are frequently drug users who are looking for pets tied outside of stores and pets in unlocked cars. They will take the pet to another neighbor and try to sell it for $10-$15.

Since you know that petnapping is on the increase, you can take precautions. Don't let your pet roam free. A dog or cat running loose several blocks from any house is the favorite victim of petnappers. Don't tie your pet in front of any store, or leave the pet in the car in shopping center parking lots. Keep your dog or cat in a secure, locked area.

By all means, have your dog tattooed with your Social Security number (on the dog's inside flank). Register your dog's number with the National Dog Registry (NDR), 227 Stebbins Road, Carmel, N.Y. 10512. The tattoo itself costs about $10. It is now done routinely at many dog shows and by veterinarians. If you have any problem locating a qualified person in your area to do the tattooing, you can write to the NDR for some names and addresses. The tattoo prevents any reputable lab from buying the pet.

Although a number of dog registry services have sprung up in recent years (it's a growth industry among entrepreneurs), many have also failed. The "Lifetime Family Memberships" ended with the business lives of the registries. We recommend the NDR because this 13-year-old pioneer in the field is so well know to labs, police departments, and dog pounds who will call this organization when a tattooed pet is found. It's in the interests of all pet owners to have one strong central registry rather than many small registries scattered around the states. (People who find a dog would have to call many different places to see if the pet were registered there.)

Note: If you do find a dog on the loose, always check the right inside flank for a tattoo. If you find one, *do not* call the Social Security office. This office can't (legally) give you the name and address of the individual whose number you've found. Instead call the NDR at (914) 277-4485. You could make a fellow dog owner very happy.

Finding a lost pet

There are several other precautionary steps you can take.

Buy a strong leather collar with a wide nameplate that is riveted onto or is part of the collar itself. Ask a jeweler to engrave your name, address, city, state, zip code and phone number on this plate. Don't put the pet's name on the collar. Once a petnapper learns the pet's name, he may be able to coax the pet to follow him. Don't bother to buy the name tags that hook onto collars. They can rub against rabies and other metal tags, and your name and address could soon become illegible.

Another important precaution: Set up a pet file. This file should include two color photographs of your pet—a head-on shot and a profile shot of the whole pet which shows any prominent color markings. Keep the color negative in the file. Now write a brief description of your pet: age, sex, breed, noticeable scars, and height (as measured from the floor to the top of the pet's shoulder). Add a record of rabies vaccination and a veterinarian's health certificate. Keep this file handy at home. If you do go traveling with your pet, take this file just as you would carry your own passport. You can use the page at the end of this chapter to start a pet file.

Six steps to take if your pet is lost

Lost from your home

1. Have "LOST PET" notices printed at one of the instant print shops in your neighborhood. This notice should contain information from your pet file: age, sex, breed, prominent marking and scars. Again, *don't* include the pet's name. Offer a "large reward" but don't specify an amount. Tell approximately when and where you last saw your pet. Give your name, address and phone number. Say that you will accept collect calls. You can type this notice or simply hand print it clearly. You should simultaneously run off a number of color photographs of your pet and mount this picture to the printed sheet. Or if this isn't practical or too time-consuming, give the instant printer a copy of your picture. He can reduce its size and have it printed right on the sheet for a small extra charge.

Distribute this "LOST PET" notice immediately to:

- The mailman
- Neighborhood children
- Local police, particularly any animal control officers
- Humane societies, dog pounds and other dog/cat collection agencies
- Newspaper delivery boys
- Local veterinarians

Post this notice on:

- Local school bulletin boards
- Supermarket and drug store message centers
- Neighborhood lamp posts

Note:

Here's one method which can be very effective. Go to a printer or a small company which specializes in direct mail (usually listed in the Yellow Pages under "Advertising—Direct Mail" or "Mailing Shops"). Ask the company to do a Zip Code mailing to the area where your pet was lost. That means every family who lives in that area will be informed about your lost pet. *Field & Stream* magazine tells how a Labrador owner named Bill Connor used this method after all else had failed and his dog had been missing for *sixty days* in Lincoln, Nebraska. A local mailing service sent out 5,000 notices for him in that Zip Code area. The saturation worked. Bill received a call in Michigan that his Labrador had been found. The notice had reached a man who had taken the Lab in, thinking it was one of the dogs he owned. The notice and identifications convinced him otherwise. Some dog experts note that many lost dogs *never travel more than 1½ miles from the point where they are lost*. Concentrate your mailing on this area.

2. Assuming that you have tattooed and registered your dog, call the NDR at (914) 277-4485 and report your pet missing.

3. *Visit* (do not call) all animal pounds in your area, as well as in neighboring areas. A phone call is useless because the animal center may have dozens of pets that match the description of your pet. After inspecting the dogs or cats, always leave one of your "LOST PET" notices. Leave at least two phone numbers where you can be reached. People who leave only mail addresses at the pounds may not be contacted for several days after the pet is found.

4. Place an ad in your local newspaper, similar in wording to your "LOST PET" notice. But since you can't include a picture, be sure to describe your pet carefully. Example:

"LOST B & W CAT, mixed breed with some Persian. White hourglass mark on back. Small half-inch scar under right eye. Lost Sat., July 8, in vicinity of Grand and Merrimac. Large reward (202) 987-3312 collect."

As noted, dog- and catnappers regularly read these columns looking for "reward" notices. They believe (correctly) that an owner will pay more than a lab or a breeder farm. If someone calls you and says that they "bought a cat that sounds like yours from some man on the street," don't turn detective. It could be true. Also your primary goal must be to get your pet back in good health, not to nab the petnapper—as satisfying as that would be.

5. Call one of the local radio stations* which subscribes to the National Pet Patrol. Some 600 stations across the country will broadcast a free announcement about pets lost and found in their areas. Even if you don't reach a Pet Patrol subscriber, many other stations may also air a lost dog or cat notice free of charge.

6. Continue to visit pounds and animal collection centers. Sometimes a person who has temporarily adopted your pet on the street may grow tired of it and release it or turn it in to a pound weeks later. Involve the whole family in spreading the "LOST PET" notices. Remember that all of this search activity is much better than grieving or blaming yourself for having left a gate

---

*If you would like a free directory to the 600 stations that belong to the Pet Patrol, write to Pet Patrol, The American Humane Association, P.O. Box 1266, Denver, Colo. 80201. It's a very handy folder to have should you lose your pet.

ajar. It also can almost double your chances of finding your lost friend.

Lost on the road

If your pet turns up missing while you are traveling, you can still follow many of the six steps just described. However, you now have the added problem that you may only be passing through an area, and you have to return to work.

If you have carried your pet file with you, it will still be relatively simple to run off the "LOST PET" notices. But specify next to your phone number the date on which you will be back home. It is essential that you note that you will accept collect calls. Be sure to take these notices to hotels and motels along the route, particularly the last one you stayed in before your pet disappeared. Your pet may return to this hotel.

How to search for a dog or cat lost in the woods

The most effective search technique devised is the same used to find lost people—grid search. This involves having a group of people follow a search pattern in a particular area, and eliminates the hit-or-miss chaos of a disorganized search.

When your dog or cat is lost in the woods, round up the family and as many nearby campers as you can recruit. Form a single line similar to the diagram at right.

Space the searchers 100-, 60- or 20-feet apart. While you cover considerably less territory, the 20-foot spacing is the most thorough. There is approximately a 50% chance that searchers spaced 100-feet apart could miss an unconscious dog or cat. How far you space the searchers also depends on the line-of-sight conditions. In an open area, the searchers can be relatively far apart. In dense woods, they should be close together.

The search members on each outer edge should mark the outer limits of the search pattern by putting out biodegradable markers, such as pieces of newspaper. When the line of march reaches the end of a particular area, the outside flank searcher leads the pivoting line (SEE DIAGRAM). This person from the

Finding a lost pet

far left pivots around the search area, beginning just to his right of the marked line as the group walks back in the adjacent area.

Remember that a frightened or injured pet may make no sound when called. You must watch carefully and make a second sweep over the same area. Many lost dogs are found within 1½ miles of the point where they were lost.

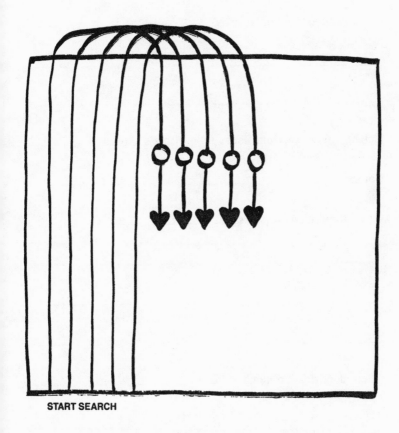

START SEARCH

*Grid search patterns. Searchers pivot
at end of search area and move into
next section. (See text.)*

Use this page within the book to set up your own Pet File. It can be of real help if your pet is ever lost.

Name of pet _____

Birthday _____

Breed or breed mixtures _____

_____

_____

Height (measured from floor to top of pet's shoulder) _____

Colors _____

Unusual markings or scars _____

_____

_____

_____

Tatoo identification number _____

Hair is: ☐ LONG   ☐ SHORT

Date this information was recorded _____

Head Shot

(Paste color photo in this area)

Profile Shot of Whole Pet

(Paste color photo in this area)

10

WHAT YOU SHOULD KNOW ABOUT U.S. AND FOREIGN PET TRAVEL

U.S. and foreign pet travel

Your pet can become a welcome guest in almost any part of the world if you take the time to learn the local attitudes and laws which affect them.

Local ordinances bar dogs and cats from most restaurants and grocery stores in the U.S. But in France, a friendly poodle sitting under its owner's chair in a cafe is a common sight. Dogs and cats are welcomed everywhere in Italy, but you must muzzle dogs if on a leash longer than one meter (3.3 feet). In the Netherlands you can wander through most stores and restaurants with your pet without ever being stopped, except by people who want to ask questions about the pet or tell you about theirs. In most parts of the world you can ride public transportation if you have a small pet which is kept in its carrier.

Dog and cat foods are not in universal supply all over the world. You may look in vain for your pet's favorite brand and have to make substitutes.

Pets are not allowed in Russian hotels, but if you're staying with friends in a private home you'll be relieved to know that pets can travel on public transportation and railroads.

Local ordinances in some areas of the states and overseas may also require you to clean up after your pet or to walk your pet only in designated ateas. If you're traveling overseas, call the American consulate and ask about local laws that affect pet owners. You can get the same information in the U.S. from the local office of the A.S.P.C.A.

A little knowledge can keep you and your pet out of hot water.

You can cross state lines all over the U.S. with dogs and cats with virtually no problem. However, if you go to Hawaii your pet will be quarantined for 120 days, and you pick up the bill—$220 for dogs, $180 for cats.

Wherever you travel, you should always carry with you the Veterinarian Health Certificate and a Rabies Vaccination Certificate. The latter is very important if your pet should bite a person or another animal. Unless you carry proof that your pet has been inoculated against rabies, you pet could be impounded for ten days or more.

If you travel to Canada, a healthy cat will be admitted without any papers. Dogs must have a rabies certificate issued during the previous twelve months. Ironically you face a much tougher grilling when you return to the U.S. If your dog appears sickly, it will be examined at the border by a U.S. veterinarian (at your expense). You will have to carry proof of the type of rabies vaccination your pet has had (usually on the Rabies Vaccination Certificate). For example, if "Chick Embryo" vaccine was used, your dog must have been inoculated not less than one month before—and not more than three years before arrival at the U.S. border. If "Nerve Tissue" vaccine was used, it must not have been given less than one month—or more than one year prior to arrival.

When traveling to Mexico with your pets, you must make advance preparation. You mail a health certificate (in duplicate) to the Mexican consulate in your city or area, along with a $4 fee. The certificate must include the following: a description of your pet, number of the rabies vaccine used, distemper vaccine, and a veterinarian's statement that the animal is free of infectious diseases.

Important

Always carry your pet's medical papers (as mentioned above) when traveling in a foreign country. You can check some of the current regulations of foreign countries in this chapter. But it's still a good idea to check with the consultates of the various countries before you go to see if there have been any changes. (Changes may occur suddenly if there is an outbreak of a particular disease that the country is trying to curb.) In certain instances (fortunately rare) your pet could be destroyed if it arrives in some countries without proper documentation.

Some entrance requirements also require advance preparation. Austria, for example, requires that you have the pet's certificate of health translated into German. Other countries require photos of the pets.

U.S. and foreign pet travel

Requirements for Traveling in the 50 States of the USA

	Health certificate	Rabies inoculation	Within this time	Puppies	Other
Alabama	*	**	6 mo.	3 mo.	3,6
Alaska	*	**	6 mo.	4 mo.	6
Arizona	*	**	1 yr. kv 3 yr. mlv	4 mo.	2

Code definition

*—Health certificate required
**—Rabies inoculation required
Time—rabies inoculation must be given within the time listed
MLV—modified live virus vaccine
KV—killed virus vaccine
CEV—chick embryo vaccine
NTV—nerve tissue vaccine
Puppies—are exempt from rabies vaccination requirement up to age listed

Other

1—show dogs exempt
2—dogs from rabies quarantine area not admitted
3—dogs with screwworms not admitted
4—may be quarantined 60 days if from rabies area
5—dogs from rabies quarantine area may enter with written permit
6—not admitted if exposed to rabies or from an area where rabies exists
7—cats require health certificate and rabies vaccination
8—hunting dogs must receive rabies vaccination within 30 days of entry
9—proof of ownership required
10—puppies under 4 months from a quarantine area need a permit from Bureau of Animal Industry
11—cats must be free from contagious disease
12—cats require a health certificate
13—dogs suspected of having rabies or being bitten by a suspected rabid animal may be quarantined 60 days.

	Health certificate	Rabies inoculation	Within this time	Puppies	Other
Arkansas	*	**	1 yr.	3 mo.	2,6,7
California	*	**	30 mo. mlv	4 mo.	
Colorado	*	**	1 yr.	3 mo.	6,7
Connecticut	*	**	6 mo.		1,2,6
Delaware	*	**		4 mo.	1,5,11
Florida	*	**	6 mo.		11
Georgia	*	**	6 mo.	3 mo.	2,6
Hawaii	120-day quarantine at owner's expense				
Idaho	*	**	6 mo. ntv 2 yr. cev	4 mo.	2,6,10
Illinois	*	**	6 mo. kv 1 yr. mlv	16 wks.	
Indiana	*	**	mlv or equal duration 1 yr.	3 mo.	7
Iowa	*	**	3 yr. mlv 1 yr. kv	6 mo.	1,12
Kansas	*	**	1 yr.	3 mo.	
Kentucky	*	**	1 yr. kv 2 yr. mlv	4 mo.	1,2,6,7
Louisiana	*	**	2 yr. cev 1 yr. ntv	2 mo.	
Maine		**	mlv		

Maryland	*	**	1 yr.	4 mo.	2,6
Massachusetts	*	**	1 yr.	6 mo.	1
Michigan	*	**	6 mo. kv		1,4
Minnesota	*	**	1 yr. kv 2 yr. mlv	6 mo.	5,6
Mississippi	*	**	6 mo.	3 mo.	2,7
Missouri	*	**	2 yr. mlv 1 yr. kv	4 mo.	
Montana	*	**	2 yr. mlv	3 mo.	5
Nebraska	*	**	2 yr. mlv 1 yr. kv	4 mo.	
Nevada	*	**	2 yr. ntv 1 yr. ntv	4 mo.	1,5
New Hampshire	*	**	3 yr. cev 1 yr. kv	3 mo.	2,6
New Jersey	*				1,2,6
New Mexico	*	**	1 yr.	3 mo.	7,14
New York	*				1
North Carolina	*	**	1 yr.	4 mo.	1,5
North Dakota	*	**	3 yr. mlv	3 mo.	1,2,6,8
Ohio		**	3 yr. cev 1 yr. other	6 mo.	
Oklahoma	*	**	1 yr.		2,6

	Health certificate	Rabies inoculation	Within this time	Puppies	Other
Oregon	*	**	2 yr. mlv 6 mo. kv	4 mo.	5,12
Pennsylvania					9
Rhode Island	*	**	6 mo. kv 2 yr. mlv	6 mo. All Dogs	2,6
South Carolina	*	**	1 yr.		2,6,12
South Dakota	*	**	1 yr.		
Tennessee	*	**	1 yr.		2,6
Texas	*	**	6 mo.		
Utah	*	**		4 mo.	7
Vermont	*	**	1 yr. mlv	4 mo.	2,7
Virginia	*	**	1 yr.	4 mo.	2,6,7
Washington	*	**	2 yr. mlv 1 yr. kv	4 mo.	12
West Virginia	*	**	1 yr.	6 mo.	1,2,6,7
Wisconsin	*	**	3 yr. cev 1 yr. other	6 mo.	
Wyoming	*	**	2 yr. cev 1 yr. mlv	4 mo.	2,6
District of Columbia		**	1 yr.	3 mo.	13

(Reprinted with the permission of *The American Society for the Prevention of Cruelty to Animals.*)

REQUIREMENTS FOR PET TRAVEL ABROAD

(Some of the medical requirements are very technical. Your veterinarian can explain if you have any questions. "NA" means information is not available.)

AFGHANISTAN
* Obtain (at point of origin) a certificate of rabies vaccination. Not required for cats.

ALBANIA
* Obtain (at point of origin) a veterinarian certificate of good health.

ALGERIA
* Obtain (at point of origin) a veterinarian certificate of rabies vaccination.

ANGOLA
NA

ARGENTINA
* Obtain certificates of good health and rabies inoculation from a veterinarian.
* Have these documents visaed by the Argentinian Consul.

AUSTRALIA
Entry prohibited from U.S., except Hawaii. Dogs and cats arriving from Hawaii require:
* Certificate of good health.
* Declaration from veterinarian that rabies have not existed in Hawaii for at least five years
* Declaration of residency and import permit. Apply to Chief Quarantine Officer (Animals), Dept. of Primary Industries, William Street, Brisbane, Australia.
* Animal must travel in a sealed container.
* Nine months quarantine required in Brisbane.

NOTE: If arriving from countries other than the U.S., check requirements with nearest Australian consulate.

AUSTRIA
* Obtain a certificate of good health issued by a veterinarian on his own stationery. This document should be in German or

translated into German and must provide the following information: owner's name and address, detailed identification of animal, its health status and vaccination history. (Rabies/lyssa inoculation must have been administered at least 30 days and not more than twelve months before arrival in Austria.)

BAHAMAS
* Obtain an import permit. Apply at least a month in advance to Ministry of Agriculture & Fisheries, P.O. Box N-3028, Nassau, Bahamas.
* Obtain a certificate of good health from a veterinarian within 24 hours of departure.
* Animals over six months of age require certificate of rabies inoculation (a minimum of 10 days old, maximum of nine months).

NOTE: The regulations above apply when arriving from the U.S., Canada and countries assumed to be rabies-free. Arrivals prohibited from areas having rabies.

BAHRAIN
* Obtain certificates of good health and rabies vaccination.
* If arriving from Great Britain, apply to the Ministry of Agriculture and Fisheries for a certificate affirming that the animal does not have rabies.

BANGLADESH
* Obtain a certificate of good health from a veterinarian.
* Obtain an import license.

BARBADOS
* Obtain an importation and transshipment permit from the Ministry of Agriculture, Barbados. Direct importation is permitted to animals arriving from: Ireland, Great Britain, Jamaica, Nevis, Anguilla, St. Kitts, St. Lucia and St. Vincent.

NOTE: Entry is not permitted if arriving from a country where rabies has been reported (includes U.S. and Canada). Contact nearest Barbadian consulate for additional information.

U.S. and foreign pet travel

BELGIUM
* Obtain a certificate of good health (in Dutch, English, French or German) authorized by the Veterinary Service in the country of origin. This document must include complete description of animal, owner's name and the address at destination and state: that vaccination against rabies has been completed and applied with one of the following: an inactivated nerve-tissue vaccine, the live vaccine of the type Flury "High Egg Passage" (HEP), the live vaccine of the type Flury "Low Egg Passage" (LEP) or a tissue grown vaccine on the basis of the Era-tribe. Your veterinarian will explain.

NOTE: Vaccinations have certain time limits depending on type and age of animal:
1. Vaccinations given to animals after 3 months of age must have been applied at least one month but not more than six months prior to shipment (or one year if HEP-vaccine applied).
2. If LEP-vaccine or the Era-tribe type is applied, the vaccine is valid only if given (to animals over three months of age) at least one month but not more than two years prior to transport.

Import from African countries must be cleared with Belgian Ministry of Agriculture. No restriction in import from Netherlands or Luxembourg. Rabies vaccination not required from Great Britain.

BELIZE
* Obtain certificates of good health and rabies vaccination from a veterinarian.

NOTE: Import possible only from U.S.A

BERMUDA
* Obtain a certificate of good health from a veterinarian within ten days before arrival. This document must indicate:

1. breed, sex, age and color of animal
2. that the animal is free from external parasites and communicable diseases.
3. has not been exposed to rabies and has not been in an area where rabies exists (in the last six months).
4. has received rabies inoculations since three months old and

that the last inoculation was administered at least one month and not longer than twelve months before arrival.

* Obtain an import permit from the Director of Agriculture & Fisheries, Point Finger Road, Paget, Bermuda.

* Obtain a document attesting that the animal did not reside during the thirty miles of any area known to be infected with foot and mouth disease.

NOTE: If arriving direct from New Zealand, Australia, Great Britain or Jamaica, rabies inoculation is not required.

BENIN
* Obtain (at point of origin) veterinarian certificates of good health and rabies vaccination.

BHUTAN
NA

BOLIVIA
* Obtain from a veterinarian (at the point of origin) a certificate of good health.

BOTSWANA
NA

BRAZIL
* Obtain a certificate of good health from a veterinarian.
* Have this document authorized by the Brazilian consulate before departure.

BRUNEI
* Obtain an import license before departure from the Agricultural Dept.
* Obtain from a veterinarian (at the point of origin) certificates of rabies vaccination and good health.
* 180 days quarantine is required and accommodations avail-

U.S. and foreign pet travel

ability should be checked beforehand with the State Veterinary Officer, Office of the Director of Agriculture, Brunei.

NOTE: Animals from Australia, New Zealand, Ireland, Sabah, Sarawak, Singapore and Great Britain are exempt from quarantine.

BULGARIA
* Obtain a certificate of good health and rabies vaccination. This document must be issued by a veterinarian at the point of origin at least one month and not more than twelve months prior to shipment (six months prior for cats).

BURMA
* Obtain a certificate of good health.

BURUNDI
* Not more than 15 days prior to departing, obtain an import permit and a certificate of good health from a veterinarian at the point of origin. The latter must specify: country or origin, owner's full name and address, animal's sex, species, that it is free from ticks, has not been exposed to contagious diseases and has received a rabies inoculation over one month (but less than one year) before departing if an activated or Kelev vaccine has been given; 36 months prior if Flury vaccine has been given.
* A veterinarian will inspect the animal upon arrival.

CAMEROON
* Less than 48 hours prior to departure obtain certificates of good health and rabies inoculation from a veterinary authority.

CANADA
* Animals from the U.S. require a certificate of rabies inoculation stating that this vaccination was given with 36 months prior to departure.

NOTE: Check with consulate for regulations regarding arrival from other countries.

CANARY ISLANDS
Regulations same as those for entry to Spain.

CAPE VERDE ISLANDS
* Obtain a certificate of good health from a veterinarian.
* Dogs also require a certificate of rabies vaccination.

CAYMAN ISLANDS
* Obtain permit from the Dept. of Agriculture, Cayman Islands.

CENTRAL AFRICAN EMPIRE
* Obtain a certificate from a veterinarian that states:
  a. rabies vaccination was given at least 2 weeks but not more than six months prior to arrival.
  b. rabies did not exist in the area where the animal was residing in the 60 days prior to transport.

CHAD
* Obtain (at the point of origin) a certificate of good health from a veterinarian.
* Obtain a certificate of rabies inoculation.

CHILE
* Obtain a good health certificate from a public agency in the country of origin. From the same agency, obtain a certificate of rabies vaccination for dogs.
* Have the above documents legalized at the Chilean consulate.

CHINA (People's Republic)
* Obtain from a veterinarian (at the point of origin) a certificate of good health and rabies vaccination.

COLOMBIA
* Obtain an import license from the Ministry of Agriculture with the I.C.A stamp.
* Obtain a good health certificate and have it visaed at the Argentinian consulate in the country of origin. This document must attest that distemper and rabies vaccinations have been given at least 8 days prior to shipment (and not more than three years before).
* Manager of airline carrying the animal must be notified in advance (at disembarkation location) in order to arrange the presence of a veterinarian upon animal's arrival.

COMORES ISLANDS
NA

CONGO (People's Republic)
* Obtain a certificate from a veterinarian certifying that a rabies vaccination was given at least three weeks and not more than six months before arrival in Congo and that for at least 60 days before the animal was transported no cases of rabies existed.

COOK ISLANDS
NA

COSTA RICA
* Obtain an import permit from the Veterinary Health Dept., San Jose, Costa Rica.
* From a government veterinarian obtain:
  1. a certificate stating that the animal is in good health and has been vaccinated against rabies.
  2. a certificate of Taenia Echionoccoccus vaccination.
* Have these certificates legalized at the Costa Rican consulate.

CUBA
* Obtain from a government veterinarian (at the point of origin) a good health certificate, and for dogs, a certificate of rabies vaccination.
* All documents must be authorized at Cuban consulate before departure.

CYPRUS
* Obtain an import license from the Director of Veterinary Services.
* Quarantine upon arrival is required for all animals; dogs will be quarantined for six months at owner's expense.

CZECHOSLOVAKIA
* Obtain a certificate of good health and rabies vaccination from a government veterinary agency. This document must be obtained a minimum of two days (maximum 21 days) prior to disembarkment, and it must certify that no contagi-

ous diseases existed in the animal's place of residency and no rabies existed.

* Manager of transporting airlines, at office in Czechoslovakia, must be notified at least 24 hours in advance of animal's arrival so that a veterinarian will be on hand to examine it.

DENMARK
* Obtain a certificate of good health and rabies innoculation which gives complete identification of animal. (Inoculation must have been given at least 4 weeks but not more than one year prior to arrival in Denmark.

NOTE: The above regulations apply to the U.S., Greenland and countries where rabies exist. Check with the consulate if in doubt about requirements.

DJOBPITO (Rep.)
* Obtain a certificate of rabies inoculation for animals over 6 months old. (Inoculation must have been given at least 4 weeks but not more than twelve months prior to shipment).

DOMINICAN REPUBLIC
* Obtain (before departure) a certificate of good health from a veterinarian licensed by the government.

EGYPT
* Obtain a certificate of good health from a government veterinarian at the point of origin (at least two weeks before intended arrival).

EL SALVADOR
* Obtain an import permit before departure. Apply to Animal Quarantine Dept., San Salvador, enclosing a certificate of good health and rabies inoculation that has been validated by the Salvadorean consulate.

EQUATORIAL GUINEA
* Obtain a certificate of rabies vaccination.

ETHIOPIA
* Before departure obtain a certificate of good health from a veterinarian.

U.S. and foreign pet travel

FIJI
* Dogs and cats prohibited entry into Fiji by air except those imported from New Zealand, New South Wales, Tasmania, Victoria and South Australia. Check requirements with consulate.

FINLAND
* Obtain importation permission from Ministry of Agriculture, Helsinki.
* Obtain a veterinarian certificate of good health before shipment.

FRANCE
Required documents must be issued by an authorized veterinarian at the point of origin.
1. If 12 months old or more:
   * certificate of good health obtained not more than five days before transport. This document must attest that the country of origin was rabies-free in the last 36 months and that the animal has lived there since birth or during the last six months.
2. over three months of age;
   * certificate of good health or rabies inoculation as outlined in number one.
3. Dogs must be vaccinated against distemper and hepatitis a minimum of one month (maximum 12 months) prior to transport (revaccination valid if given within one year prior to transport).
4. Cats must obtain a certificate of inoculation against typhus (minimum of one month, maximum 12 months prior to transport).
5. Animals younger than three months are denied entry.

FRENCH GUIANA
Entry requirements same as for France.

FRENCH WEST INDIES
Entry requirements same as for France.

GABON
* No requirements if under three months of age.
* Certificate from a veterinarian (issued in country of origin

less than three days prior to transport) or certificate of rabies inoculation.

GAMBIA
* Obtain an import permit from the Principal Veterinary Officer, Banjul.
* Obtain (at point of origin) a veterinarian certificate of good health.

GERMANY (East)
* Obtain a certificate of good health from the government veterinary agency (maximum of five days before trip).
* Obtain a certificate of rabies vaccination. Two copies of this document are required and must be obtained at least a month but not more than a year prior to the trip. This must be authorized by country of origin's veterinary service.
* Animal must pass health exam at entry point.
* Obtain an import license if stay will exceed 28 days.

GERMANY (West)
* Obtain a certificate of good health. This must be written in German (or translated into German) on the stationery of a licensed veterinarian in the country of origin. The following information must be included: animal's name, race, sex, age, colour, the date of health exam, and that the animal is disease-free, and that in the last three months rabies has not been reported within a 13 mile radius. This certificate is valid for 10 days if importation is from Europe, 20 days if arriving from a non-European country.

NOTE: Exemption from the above regulations is granted if the animal is used professionally, by an artist, a seeing-eye dog, a service dog (with German military, customs or lifesavings organization) or is in transit (may not leave airport in this case).

GHANA
NA

GIBRALTAR
NA

GILBERT ISLANDS
NA

GREECE
* Obtain a certificate of rabies vaccination and good health. This document must be issued by a veterinary authority before departing country of residency and must attest that the rabies vaccination was made not more than a year (six months for cats) and not under six days before arriving.
* Submit animal to health clearance upon entry.

GRENADA
* Obtain a certificate of good health.
* Obtain an "entry authority" from the Government Veterinarian, St. George's, Grenada.

GUAM
* Obtain, up to ten days prior to trip, a certificate of good health.
* Have in possession a certificate of rabies vaccination authorized by a veterinarian within six months prior to trip.
* Animal is subject to up to 120 days quarantine (at owner's expense). Obtain a letter that confirms arrangements for quarantine have been made with Animal Quarantine Station, Dept. of Agriculture, Government of Guam, Agana, Guam 91910.

NOTE: The above quarantine regulation will be waived if animal arrives from Australia, Great Britain, Hawaii or New Zealand and is accompanied by a notarized document stating that the animal was born in one of these countries and resided there for at least 120 days before transport.

GUATEMALA
* Obtain (at point of origin) a certificate of good health from a government licensed veterinarian.

GUINEA-BISSAU
* Obtain a certificate of good health from a veterinarian before departure.

GUINEA
* Obtain a veterinarian's certificate of good health and rabies vaccination.

GUYANA
* Obtain a certificate of good health.
* Obtain an import permit from Ministry of Agriculture.

NOTE: If arriving from a rabies-infected country, quarantine for three months at owner's expense is imposed.

HAITI
* Obtain a certificate of good health from a veterinarian.
* For dogs, certificate of rabies vaccination also required.

HONDURAS
* Obtain an import permit from Direccion General de Ganaderia Y Veterinaria (this can be arranged upon arrival).
* Obtain a certificate of good health from a veterinarian and have it legalized at the Honduras Consulate before departure.
* Certificate of rabies inoculation, distemper and hepatitis is also required for dogs.

HONG KONG
* Obtain an import permit in advance of trip from Agriculture & Fisheries Dept., Canton Road Government Offices, 393 Canton Road, 12th Floor, Kowloon, Hong Kong. When applying for this document include the animal's species, breed, age, sex, color, owner's name and address, expected arrival date in Hong Kong and how arriving (plane, train, etc.)
* Obtain a certificate of good health from the government veterinary authority of the country of origin. This is not valid if obtained more than 2 weeks prior to departure date.

NOTE: Upon arrival the animal must be quarantined at a kennel designated for this purpose. Quarantine is six months unless arriving from Australia, Ireland, New Zealand or Great Britain. Animals from these countries may have quarantine waived if the following are presented: certificate attesting that the animal was living in one of the aforementioned countries for at least six months prior to arrival in Hong Kong, a certificate of good health obtained from an official veterinarian of the government of country of origin, a document from captain of transporting plane or ship that the animal traveled isolated from other animals.

U.S. and foreign pet travel

HUNGARY

* Obtain a certificate of good health (in country of origin) from the veterinary health authority. This must be obtained at least 8 days before trip and certify that the animal is healthy, has been vaccinated against rabies (and distemper inoculation required for dogs) and that no rabies cases were reported with 20 km. of the point of origin with the three months before transport.

ICELAND

* Must obtain an import license (contact Ministry of Agriculture, Arnarhvolur, Reykjavik).

INDIA

* Obtain a certificate of good health and rabies inoculation from a veterinarian in the country of origin. This must be issued at least 7 days before arrival in India.
* Make arrangements to be met at airport by a veterinarian authorized by the government. He must issue a document certifying that the animal is in good health.

INDONESIA

* Obtain two certificates of good health 5 days before transport. These must certify that the animal is disease-free and was not in an area infected with yellow fever at least five days before departure.
* Arrange with carrier's office to be met at airport by a veterinarian.
* Obtain a certificate certifying that a rabies vaccination was given at least 12 months before transport.

NOTE: Pets are prohibited entry to Palembang, Bali & Irian Barat.

IRAN

* Obtain (in the country of origin) a certificate of good health and rabies vaccination from a veterinarian.
* Have this document authorized at the Iranian consulate prior to departure.

IRAQ

* Obtain a certificate of good health from a veterinian.

IRELAND

* Obtain an import license from the Dept. of Agriculture, Veterinary Section, Agriculture House, Kildare St., Dublin 2.
* Air transportation permitted by air freight only.
* Quarantine is required at owner's expense. The animal will receive two rabies inoculations during this time.

ISRAEL

* Obtain a certificate of good health and rabies vaccination from a veterinarian.

NOTE: An unvaccinated dog may enter but must be vaccinated within two weeks of arrival. Dogs from Asia and Africa are quarantined for one month and revaccinated during that time.

ITALY

* Obtain from veterinary authority (in country of origin) a certificate of good health and rabies vaccination. This must be authorized at least four weeks but a maximum of one year (six months for cats) before departure.
* Dogs require muzzle if being led on a chain over one meter in length.

IVORY COAST

* Obtain a certificate of good health and rabies vaccination. This document must certify that no diseases existed in area of origin during the six weeks prior to transport.

NOTE: If the animal is not arriving with a passenger, an import license is also required (unless arriving from Benin, Chad, France, Congo, Central African Republic, Upper Volta, Malagasy Republic, Mali, Gabon, Senegal, Niger or Mauritania).

JAMAICA

Cats and dogs prohibited except those born and bred in Great Britain and arriving directly from there.
* Obtain an import permit. Apply to Veterinary Division of the Ministry of Agriculture, Kingston, Jamaica.
* Obtain a certificate of good health which affirms that the animal received a rabies vaccination at least 6 months before transport.

U.S. and foreign pet travel

JAPAN
  * Cats do not require any documents.
  * Dogs require:
    1. Certificate of good health.
    2. Certificate of rabies vaccination obtained from the government veterinary authority at departure area.

NOTE: At least 14 days quarantine is required at owner's expense unless the animal belongs to U.S. military personnel or is arriving directly from Fiji, Finland, Australia, Great Britain, Cyprus, Iceland, Ireland, Hong Kong, Northern Ireland, New Zealand, Taiwan, Singapore, Sweden, Portugal or Norway. Quarantine varies for animals arriving from these countries.

JORDAN
  * obtain certificate of good health and rabies vaccination.

KENYA
  * Obtain an import permit from Livestock Officer, Veterinary Dept. Post Office, Kabete, Kenya. Allow at least one month from submission of application for the permit to arrive.
  * At point of origin obtain a veterinarian certificate of good health and rabies vaccination.

KOREA (Democratic People's Republic)
NA

KOREA (Republic)
  * Obtain (at point of origin) a veterinarian certificate of good health and rabies vaccination.
  * 10 days quarantine imposed.

KUWAIT
  * Obtain (at point of origin) a veterinarian certificate of good health.

LEBANON
  * In country of origin obtain a certificate of good health from a veterinarian and have it authorized by the government's veterinary agency.

LEEWARD ISLANDS
NA

LESOTHO
NA

LIBERIA

NA

LIBYA
* Obtain two documents of good health from a veterinarian.
* Obtain a certificate of rabies vaccination.

LUXEMBOURG
Requirements are the same as those for entry to Belgium. No restrictions are placed on the transportation of cats and dogs within the Benelux countries—Belgium, Netherlands, Luxembourg.

MACAO
NA

MALAGASY REPUBLIC
* Obtain in advance an import permit from the "Directeur du Service de L'Elevage et de la Peche Maritime de la Rep. Democratique Malgache"
* Obtain, at the point of origin, a certificate of good health from a veterinarian. This must be issued less than 15 days before transport and must be stamped by the regional Director of the Veterinary Services. It must state complete description of the animal, that the animal is in good health and that the area of origin has not been contaminated with any infectious diseases for a specified period of time (the import authorization will indicate what the length of time is).
* Cats over 6 months (dogs between 3 and 6 months) require document stating that it has received a rabies inoculation more than 30 days, less than 12 months, prior to transport,
* Dogs over 6 months require document stating that a rabies inoculation was given more than 30 days but less than 3 years prior to transport.
* A sanitary examination is required upon arrival and possible quarantine.

MALAWI
* Obtain a certificate of good health and rabies inoculation

from a veterinarian.

MALAYSIA
* Obtain a landing permit.
* Obtain a certificate of good health. Must be obtained one week prior to transport and must affirm that the country of origin is rabies-free and the animal was not imported there.
* Obtain an import permit from Malaysian Veterinary Dept.
* Quarantine of 30 days or longer required unless arriving from Australia, New Zealand, Singapore, Great Britain or Ireland (and if from Singapore obtain export license from Government of Singapore).
* Station manager (at disembarkation) must be given complete details on animal's arrival by the originating airport. And space should be reserved for animals requiring quarantine.

MALDIVE ISLANDS
* Dogs require an import permit. Apply to Ministry of External Affairs.

MALI
* Obtain a certificate of rabies inoculation.
* In country of origin obtain a sanitary certificate (can be obtained a maximum of three days before transport). This document must state the area of origin was free from contagious diseases for at least six weeks (and for dogs, must also state that no rabies have been known to exist for at least six weeks).

MALTA
* Importation denied to cats and dogs.

MAURITANIA
* No requirements for animals younger than 3 months.
* For other animals, obtain (in country of origin) a certificate of good health and rabies inoculation.

MAURITIUS
* Obtain prior to departure an import permit. Apply to Ministry of Agriculture and Natural Resources, Mauritius.
* Obtain (in country of origin) a sanitary certificate.
* Six months quarantine will be required upon entry.

MEXICO
* Under three months of age denied entry.
* For other animals obtain a certificate of good health and rabies inoculation from a veterinarian.
* Have this document visaed by the Mexican consul (unless it is obtained from a government agency).

MOROCCO
* Obtain (at point of origin) a veterinarian certificate of good health.

MOZAMBIQUE
* Obtain an import permit from the Directorate of Veterinary Services, Mozambique.
* Obtain a certificate of good health from a veterinarian (at point of origin).
* Obtain a certificate of rabies vaccination for animals over six months old. This document is valid only if issued not more than six months before transport.

NAURU
NA

NEPAL
* Obtain a certificate of good health and rabies vaccination from a veterinarian.

NETHERLANDS
Health certificate and rabies inoculation requirements the same as for entry to Belgium. For more information contact the nearest Netherlands Consulate.

NETHERLANDS ANTILLES
* Obtain a certificate of good health from a veterinarian and a certificate of rabies vaccination (at point of origin).

NOTE: Animals from Central and South America are denied entry—except those from Guyana and Suriname.

NEW CALEDONIA
* Entry permitted only if coming from these rabies-free countries: Australia, Bermuda, Bahamas, French Polynesia, Iceland, Ireland Republic, Fiji, New Hebrides, Reunion, New Zealand, Mauritius, Malta, American Samoa, Samoa (West-

ern), Great Britain and U.S. Virgin Islands and Jamaica.
* Apply at least 3 months in advance for an authorization from Service de l'Elevage, P.O. Box 11, Noumea. The application must state number and type of animal, race, age, sex, and exact place of origin.
* Obtain (at least 4 weeks but not more than 6 months before departure) a certificate of rabies vaccination.
* Animal is checked as cargo with air waybill and must travel on same aircraft as the accompanying passenger.

NEW ZEALAND
* Entry permitted only to animals from Australia, Great Britain and Ireland.
* Animal must be sent as cargo in a strong container. Seeing-eye dogs may travel in cabin with passenger if permission is obtained from the airline.

NICARAGUA
* Obtain (at point of origin) a certificate of good health and rabies vaccination from a veterinarian.
* Obtain an import permit from Ministerio de Agriculture Y Ganaderia, Managua.

NIGER
* Obtain a certificate of good health from a veterinarian. This must be issued not more than three days before transport and must state that the point of origin has been free from rabies and infectious diseases for at least six weeks.

NIGERIA
* Obtain an import permit.
* Obtain (at point of origin) a veterinarian certificate of good health and rabies vaccination. This document is not valid after seven days.

NIUE
NA

NORFOLK ISLAND
NA

NORWAY
* Animals arriving from Sweden and Finland require a vet-

erinarian certificate of good health (issued not more than 6 weeks prior to arrival).
* Animals from other countries require an import license. Apply to Veterinarian Directorate, Oslo. Also required is a certificate of good health obtained from a veterinarian and visaed at the Norwegian consulate.
* Quarantine of 4 weeks at owner's expense will be imposed.
* Reserve quarantine accommodations in advance: telex the station manager of transporting airline at point of disembarkation.

OMAN
NA

PAKISTAN
* Obtain a veterinarian certificate of good health.

PANAMA
* Obtain a certificate of good health from a veterinarian and obtain a certificate of rabies inoculation (not more than 16 months and not less than one month before arrival).
* Obtain an import permit from the Ministry of Agriculture of Panama City. The transporting airline can request this via telex up to 24 hours before animal's arrival.
* Quarantine imposed upon arrival at owner's expense for a period of 40 days.

PAPUA NEW GUINEA
* Animals prohibited entry by air (except from Australia).
* Obtain an import permit before transport. Apply to Chief Quarantine Officer (Animals), Dept. of Agriculture Stock and Fisheries at Port Moresby Papua New Guinea.

NOTE: Some types of dogs are denied import.

PARAGUAY
* Obtain a certificate of good health from a veterinarian.

PERU
* Obtain a veterinarian certificate of good health and rabies inoculation at point of origin.

U.S. and foreign pet travel

PHILIPPINES
* Obtain a veterinarian certificate of good health and rabies inoculation at point of origin.

PHILIPPINES
* Obtain (at point of origin) a veterinarian certificate of good health and rabies vaccination. This document must affirm that the animal has not been exposed to a contagious disease.
* Obtain an import permit in advance. Apply to Bureau of Animal Industry.
* The station manager of the transporting airlines (at point of disembarkation) must notify the Quarantine Inspector in Manila at least 24 hours in advance of the animal's expected arrival.

POLAND
* Obtain two copies of a good health certificate and a certificate of rabies vaccination. Latter must be issued at least four weeks (but not more than one year for dogs, six months for cats) before transport and must be legalized by the veterinary service of the country of origin.

PORTUGAL
* Obtain in advance an authorization from "Direccao Geral dos Servicos Pecuarios," Lisbon.
* Obtain (at point of origin) a certificate of good health from a veterinarian.
* If arriving from a country where rabies exist, obtain a certificate of rabies vaccination that states date and type of vaccination, name of the manufacturer and serial number of vaccine, the veterinarian's statement with his name, profession, signature and stamp.
* The station manager of transporting airline (at disembarkation point) must be advised in advance of animal's arrival so that a veterinarian will be on hand to meet it.

PUERTO RICO
* Obtain (at point or origin) a certificate of good health from a veterinarian. This document is valid for up to a month before arrival. For dogs, it must be stated that the animal was residing in an area free from contagious, infectious or trans-

missible disease. Dogs over 8 weeks old also require a certificate of rabies vaccination (issued within six months before arrival).

QATAR
NA

REUNION
Regulations same as those for France.

RHODESIA
* Importation of animals prohibited.

ROMANIA
* Obtain certificate of good health and rabies vaccination and have it legalized by the Veterinary Service (in country of origin). This document must be issued at least 4 weeks prior to shipment (and not more than one year before—or six months for cats).

RWANDA
* Obtain a veterinarian certificate of good health at the point of origin.
* Have the animal vaccinated—Flury HEP for cats, Flury LEP for dogs.

SAMOA (American)
* Importation of pets prohibited.

SAMOA (Western)
* Obtain an import permit from the Department of Agriculture, Apia,
* Obtain a certificate of good health from veterinarian prior to transport.

SAO TOME & PRINCIPE
NA

SAUDI ARABIA
* Importation of dogs prohibited.
* For cats, obtain two copies of a veterinarian certificate of good health plus a certificate of rabies inoculation (this must state that the vaccination was given between one year and one month prior to import).

SENEGAL
* Obtain a certificate from a veterinarian stating that a rabies vaccination was given more than four weeks and less than six months before arrival.
* Obtain a veterinarian certificate of good health less than 48 hours prior to transport.

SEYCHELLES
* Obtain an import authorization from the Veterinary Dept.
* Obtain a certificate (in English) of rabies inoculation.

SINGAPORE
* Obtain at least two weeks in advance an import permit. Apply to Director of Primary Production, City Veterinary Centre, 40 Kampong Java Road, Singapore 9.
* Obtain a certificate of good health, issued within seven days of departure by the Government Veterinary Authority.
* Either obtain a certificate of rabies inoculation or have the animal vaccinated upon arrival.
* Quarantine of at least 30 days imposed unless arriving from Great Britain, Australia or New Zealand.
* Transporting airline's agent (at Singapore) should be notified at least a day in advance of arrival, so a veterinarian will be on hand.

NOTE: The above regulations pertain to importation. Transshipment requirements differ. Contact nearest consulate for details.

SOLOMON ISLANDS
NA

SOMALIA
* Obtain (at point of origin) a veterinarian certificate of good health.

SOUTH AFRICA
* Obtain a Veterinary Import Permit from the Director of Veterinary Services, Private Bag X 138, Pretoria, 0001. Apply at least 8 weeks before planned arrival.
* Obtain a certificate of rabies inoculation. Must be issued at least three months but not more than three years before arrival.

* Obtain a certificate of good health from a veterinarian (not more than three weeks before departure).
* Station manager of transporting airline in South Africa must be telexed by boarding station and apprised of animal's arrival. A veterinary services inspector will then be on hand at airport when the animal arrives.
* Quarantine imposed if animal arrives without required documents or from a country other than Great Britain.

SPAIN
* For an animal over three months old, obtain a certificate of good health and rabies vaccination. This is valid only if issued at least four weeks but not more than one year prior to shipment.
* Have this document visaed by the Spanish Consulate.
* Animals are subject to examination by Customs Veterinarian upon arrival.

NOTE: It is advised that arrival be timed to coincide with working hours to avoid clearance delays.

SRI LANKA
* Obtain a veterinarian certificate of good health and rabies vaccination in country of origin. Have this authorized by the veterinary authority prior to transport.
* For dogs, the following must be paid upon arrival—stamp fee (CER 5) and customs fee (CER250).

SUDAN
* Obtain (at point of origin) a certificate of good health and rabies vaccination from a veterinarian.
* Obtain in advance an import permit from the Sudan Veterinary Service.

SURINAME
* Obtain a certificate of good health from a veterinarian. This is to be issued at point of origin not more than two weeks prior to transport.
* Also have the animal vacinnated against rabies at least four weeks prior to arrival.
* Animal will undergo a health examination at Paramaribo (minimum charge of SFL 5 imposed).

SWAZILAND
NA

SWEDEN
1. For animals arriving from Finland and Norway:
* Obtain a "six-week affidavit" from a veterinarian before transport.
2. For arrival from other countries:
*Obtain an import permit from Lantbrukstyrelsen, 55183 Jonkopping.
*Also obtain (in country of origin) a certificate of good health from a veterinarian.
*Animals are subject to examination and quarantine upon arrival. Quarantine of 4 months cost about $6.00 (U.S. dollars) per day.

SWITZERLAND
* Obtain a certificate (in English, German, French or Italian) from a veterinarian indicating that the animal was inoculated against rabies at least one month but not more than 12 months prior to arrival. The following information must appear on this certificate: owner's name and address, complete description of animal, age, statement of good health, date of rabies vaccination, kind of vaccine, name of producer and production number of vaccine and the veterinary surgeon's signature.

SYRIA
* Obtain (at point of origin) a veterinarian certificate of good health.

TAIWAN
* Obtain an import permit unless arriving from Australia, Hong Kong, Japan or Great Britain.
* Import permits may be obtained through any Taiwan Embassy or Consulate; about six weeks are necessary for processing. Include the following information when applying: owner's name, animal's species, age and place of birth.
* Certificate of good health and rabies vaccination also must be obtained before departure.
* Quarantine (about 2 to 3 weeks) imposed upon arrival, and owner must pay the costs.

TANZANIA
NA

THAILAND
* Obtain a certificate of good health and rabies vaccination.

TOGO
* Obtain a certificate of good health issued not more than three days prior to transport. This document must state that the animal is leaving an area free from diseases contagious to the species and rabies for at least six weeks before departure.
* Obtain an import license unless arriving from Benin, Cameroon, Central African Republic, Chad, Congo, France, French overseas departments or territories, Gabon, Ivory Coast, Kalagasy Rep., Mali, Mauritania, Niger, Senegal, Upper Volta or Zaire.

TONGA
NA

TRINIDAD & TOBAGO
* Obtain a government veterinarian certificate of good health and rabies inoculation; this must state that the animal is disease-free and that the country of origin has been free from rabies for at least the last six months.
* An entry permit must be obtained in advance: apply to Director of Agriculture, St. Clair, Trinidad.
* Station manager of transporting airline (located at disembarkation point) must be notified at least 24 hours before animal's arrival. He will arrange Government Veterinary clearance.
* Quarantine of six months or more is imposed unless arriving directly from Anguilla, Antigua, Barbados, Ireland, Jamaica, Nevis, St. Kitts, St. Vincent or Great Britain.
* Pets in transit are exempt from all requirements if continuing on same aircraft. If connecting with another flight within 24 hours, apply to Director of Agriculture, Trinidad for an intransit permit.

TUNISIA
* Obtain a certificate of good health from the veterinary authorities in the country of origin. This must affirm that the

place of origin has been free from contagious animal diseases at least 6 weeks prior to transport.
* Obtain a certificate of rabies inoculation for dogs.

TURKEY
* Obtain a certificate of good health and rabies inoculation.
* Have this document issued by the Chamber of Commerce or the Ministry of Foreign Affairs (in the country of origin) and by the Turkish Consulate.

TUVALU
NA

UGANDA
* Obtain (no more than six days prior to arrival) a certificate of good health. This must be issued by a veterinarian at the point of origin.

UNITED ARAB EMIRATES
* Obtain a certificate of good health from a veterinarian at the point of origin.

UNITED KINGDOM
For animals in transit:
* If transit will require over 4 hours, consent must be obtained in advance from Cargo Dept. of the airline involved in United Kingdom. Quarantine will be imposed and owner will have to pay high fees.

For import:
* Animal must arrive as manifested cargo in a nose & paw proof container and covered by an Air Waybill.
* Cargo Dept, at arrival station must be advised in advance of arrival and be apprised of the license number shown on the boarding document, name of shipper and owner, type of pet, date of arrival, flight of arrival and departure.
* Obtain a certificate of good health.
* Obtain a "boarding document" as proof that an import license has been issued by the Ministry of Agriculture, Fisheries and Food.
* Animals may arrive only at the following airports: LHY, LGW, GLA, EDI, PIK, MAN LBA OR BHX.

* During a six months quarantine animals will receive rabies inoculations.

NOTE: Animals cannot be shipped as baggage. Failure to comply with regulations can result in fines or destruction of animal. Consult nearest consulate for more information.

UPPER VOLTA
* Obtain a certificate of good health from a veterinarian. This document must state that a rabies vaccination was given not less than 3 weeks (or more than six months) before arrival, and that no rabies has occurred in the area of origin for at least 60 days before transport.

URUGUAY
* Obtain a certificate of good health from a veterinarian that states the animal is free from external parasites.
* Obtain a certificate of rabies vaccination stating that the inoculation was given at least one month (but not more than 12 months) prior to arrival.
* Have all documents visaed at the Uruguayan consulate and issued in French, Spanish or English.

NOTE: No documents are required if the animal is in transit and not leaving the aircraft.

USA
* Inspection conducted by veterinarian at arrival point. The owner will be charged for this examination if the animal is not in good health.
* Dogs require a veterinarian rabies vaccination certificate, including dog's identification, date of inoculation and type of vaccine. This vaccination must be given not less than one month and not more than one year prior to arrival if "Nerve Tissue" vaccine used; if "Chick Embryo" vaccine used, inoculation must be given not less than one month and not more than three years prior to arrival. Dogs arriving without the rabies vaccination certificate will be inoculated at arrival point at owner's expense and must then be confined to its home for a 30-day period.
* No rabies vaccination required for dogs under three months or for those arriving from Australia, Bahamas, Bermuda,

Fiji, Great Britain, Iceland, Ireland, Jamaica, Japan, New Zealand, Norway, Sweden, or Taiwan.
* If arriving at Hawaii, dogs and cats require quarantine up to 120 days and owner must pay required fees.

USSR
* Obtain a certificate of good health from a veterinarian authorized by the local Board of Health. This cannot be issued more than ten days before arrival at port of entry.

VENEZUELA
* Obtain from an approved Government veterinarian a certificate of good health and certificate of rabies and distemper vaccinations.
* Have all documents visaed by the Venezuelan consul.

VIETNAM
NA

VIRGIN ISLANDS (U.S.A.)
* Obtain a certificate of good health from a veterinarian not more than one month prior to transport.
* Animals must be accompanied by a document stating that a rabies inoculation was given within twelve months before transport. This certificate must affirm that no rabies has occured during the past six months within a radius of 50 miles from the point of origin.
* Animals cannot leave the airport until the animal quarantine veterinarian authorizes departure.

WINDWARD ISLANDS
NA

YEMEN ARAB REPUBLIC
* Obtain a certificate of good health from a veterinarian.
* Obtain an import permit from the Veterinary Office, Dept. of Agriculture, Yeman Arab Republic.

YEMAN (People's Democratic Republic)
* Obtain a certificate of good health from a veterinarian.
* Obtain an import permit from the Veterinary Office, Dept. of Agriculture, P.O. Box 1161, Aden.

YUGOSLAVIA
* Obtain a certificate of good health from a veterinarian. This must be legalized by the veterinary authorities at the point of origin.

ZAIRE
* Obtain a certificate of good health from a veterinarian that states the animal is free from ticks and has not been exposed to contagious diseases.
* Obtain a certificate of rabies vaccination. This document must state that this inoculation was given at least four weeks but less than one year prior to transport if an inactivated or Kelev vaccine was administered (36 months prior to transport if an avianized Flury was given). Obtain this certificate not more than 15 days prior to transport.
* Medical examination will be given upon arrival and normal veterinary fee will be charged.

ZAMBIA
* Obtain a certificate of good health from a veterinarian (at point of origin).
* Apply well in advance for an import permit. Write to Veterinary and Tsetse Control Division, Ministry of Rural Development, Lusaka.
* For dogs, obtain a certificate of rabies inoculation.

N A Not available.

Index

Index

Now that you've read *Protecting Your Pets,* you know that it contains a great deal of practical, down-to-earth advice that would help anyone keep their dog or cat safe and well.

This unique book would make just a perfect Christmas, birthday or "just thinking of you" gift.

Obtain gift copies at your bookstore, or send a check or money order for $3.95 plus 75¢ for postage and handling to:

Gieseking & Clive, Inc.
Box 716
Bronxville N.Y. 10708

About the author

Hal Gieseking is a convert to consumerism from an unexpected quarter, the world of advertising. For a number of years he supervised and wrote TV commercials and print ads for clients such as American Express, KLM Royal Dutch Airlines, the United States Travel Service, and Cunard Line. He is president of a publications design firm, Gieseking & Clive Inc., and editor of the Travel Advisor. He is also the author of the "Consumer Handbook for Travelers."

About the illustrator

Dick Kline is a New York art director for a major advertising agency. He has illustrated a children's book, "Outdoor Games." He designed a new line of men's cosmetics called WOTO, and created the world's most famous paper airplane. He has flown this plane on "CBS 60 Minutes" and "The Mike Douglas Show."

3 5282 00077 7998